BRITISH PACIFIC FLEET
1944–45

The Royal Navy in the downfall of Japan

Brian Lane Herder
Illustrated by Paul Wright

OSPREY PUBLISHING
Bloomsbury Publishing Plc
Kemp House, Chawley Park, Cumnor Hill, Oxford OX2 9PH, UK
29 Earlsfort Terrace, Dublin 2, Ireland
1385 Broadway, 5th Floor, New York, NY 10018, USA
E-mail: info@ospreypublishing.com
www.ospreypublishing.com

OSPREY is a trademark of Osprey Publishing Ltd

First published in Great Britain in 2023

A catalogue record for this book is available from the British Library.

ISBN: PB 9781472856777; eBook 9781472856760; ePDF 9781472856753; XML 9781472856784

23 24 25 26 27   10 9 8 7 6 5 4 3 2 1

Maps by bounford.com
Diagrams by Adam Tooby
Index by Fionbar Lyons
Typeset by Myriam Bell Design
Printed and bound in India by Replika Press Private Ltd.

Artist's note
Readers may care to note that the original paintings from which the colour plates in this book were
prepared are available for private sale. All reproduction copyright whatsoever is retained by the
publishers. All enquiries should be addressed to cm@marineartists.co.uk
The publishers regret that they can enter into no correspondence upon this matter.

Imperial War Museums Collections
Many of the photos in this book come from the huge collections of IWM (Imperial War Museums)
which cover all aspects of conflict involving Britain and the Commonwealth since the start of the
twentieth century. These rich resources are available online to search, browse and buy at www.iwm.org.
uk/collections.
Imperial War Museums www.iwm.org.uk

Front Cover: Art by Paul Wright, © Osprey Publishing

Osprey Publishing supports the Woodland Trust, the UK's leading woodland conservation charity.

To find out more about our authors and books visit www.ospreypublishing.com. Here you will find
extracts, author interviews, details of forthcoming events and the option to sign up for our newsletter.

CONTENTS

THE FLEET'S PURPOSE

The British Pacific Fleet (BPF) was Britain's primary contribution to the direct defeat of Japan in 1945. It is best known as the Royal Navy's Pacific counterpart to the US Fast Carrier Task Force, but this is only part of the story. A major cross-section of the Royal Navy was present and accounted for in the Pacific, including submarines, light forces, replenishment groups and shore establishment.

However, the BPF's main striking force was its fast carrier force. This fast carrier force adopted the American-style designation Task Force 57 when under the command of Admiral Raymond Spruance's US Fifth Fleet. When under the command of Admiral Bill Halsey's US Third Fleet, it was known as Task Force 37. In popular culture the BPF fast carrier force is best-remembered for sharing the unique and terrifying 1945 *kamikaze* experience alongside the Americans – the only major British force to do so.

The BPF began practice strikes against the occupied Netherlands East Indies in late 1944 and early 1945. Politics demanded the BPF be formally requested by the United States for major combat operations. This was done in time for the 1 April 1945 invasion of Okinawa, codenamed Operation *Iceberg*. The BPF operated semi-independently during *Iceberg* at the general direction of US Fifth Fleet command.

The BPF's March–May 1945 carrier strikes in support of *Iceberg* proved to be the first of the BPF's two primary campaigns. The second major campaign was against the Home Islands in summer 1945. Unlike *Iceberg*, on 16 July 1945 the BPF was fully integrated under US Third Fleet command. For one dramatic month four British fast carriers and battleship *King George V* would bombard the Japanese homeland alongside the Americans.

Additionally, the BPF alone represented the British Empire at the 2 September 1945 Tokyo Bay surrender ceremony, with BPF commander-in-chief Admiral Bruce Fraser signing the surrender instrument on behalf of the British government. Afterwards, the BPF was Britain's vanguard for implementing the post-war peace.

These chores helped wrap down the war and involved returning to defeated British colonies and re-establishing British authority, taking local Japanese surrenders, repatriating Allied prisoners-of-war languishing in Japanese prison camps and helping organize the return of Japanese soldiers to their homeland. The BPF proved to be Britain's last great military formation assigned to defend the British Empire east of Suez.

Although the Royal Navy and US Navy operated alongside each other in almost every theatre at some point, coordination between the two navies on an operational and tactical level peaked in the 1945 Pacific campaign. Although not without its peaks and valleys, this wartime legacy of British and American political and naval cooperation continued and strengthened during the Cold War and continues to the current day.

The Pacific War ended well before the BPF could fully flower as a major national fleet. If the war had lasted into late 1945 as nearly everyone expected, the BPF would have more than doubled in size, and although still much smaller than its American counterpart, the BPF would have grown considerably in comparison. At nine front-line carriers, four modern battleships, 450 carrier aircraft and hundreds of additional warships and auxiliaries, the BPF would have been large and powerful enough to engage in truly independent operations. In addition, the scheduled invasion of Japan would have provided plenty of headlines and casualties to permanently sear the BPF into British national consciousness. That none of this happened was a great fortune to all involved. It also meant the Royal Navy's most powerful fleet ever would unfairly be relegated to a small corner of history.

Derived from a photograph of the event, *The Arrival of the American Fleet to Scapa Flow* documents the arrival of US Battleship Division Nine to the Royal Navy's Grand Fleet on 7 December 1917. The institutional memory of the American division joining the main British fleet would inform concepts behind the British Pacific Fleet many years later. (NHHC NH 58841-KN)

THE MISSION

Japan unleashed its shattering Far East blitzkrieg on 8 December 1941. Within mere weeks the Japanese had fully conquered the British territories of Hong Kong, Malaya, Singapore and Burma, throwing 24.1 million British Empire subjects under sudden Japanese domination. A further 190,000 Commonwealth prisoners-of-war were forced into a brutal captivity.

On 10 December 1941, Japanese naval aviation forces destroyed the Royal Navy's Singapore-based Force Z, comprising the battleship *Prince of Wales* and battlecruiser *Repulse*. The following spring, 1942, five of the six Japanese carriers that had struck Pearl Harbor rampaged through the Indian Ocean. The Royal

A rare view of five British Pacific Fleet carriers at Leyte-Samar's San Pedro Bay. From front to back: fleet carriers HMS *Victorious* and HMS *Formidable*, maintenance carrier HMS *Unicorn*, and fleet carriers HMS *Indefatigable* and HMS *Indomitable*. San Pedro Bay was the BPF's main advanced base through most of 1945. (IWM MH 5309)

Navy's Far East forces were clearly outmatched, and they withdrew across the Indian Ocean to relative safety at Madagascar.

However, by early 1943, American naval action had destroyed much of Japan's carrier striking force. Shortly afterwards, the Allies' September 1943 defeat of Fascist Italy allowed the first opportunity for the Royal Navy to send a reasonable naval reinforcement to Asia. That same month, Admiral James Somerville's Eastern Fleet advanced back to its former base at Ceylon to commence more aggressive operations against the Japanese.

At the Cairo Conference in November 1943 the combined Anglo-American high command finalized their European grand strategy to invade North-West Europe, relegating all other theatres and operations to secondary importance. Because air cover for the invasion could be provided from England, this would immediately make the Royal Navy's front-line fleet carriers redundant in the war against Germany. This force could be partially available in March 1944. US Pacific planners, however, were aware that the American war against Japan was accelerating in unpredictable fashion. They worried that substituting combined Anglo-American planning for what had essentially been unilateral American action would slow the Pacific War's increasing momentum. However, outright refusal of British assistance would cause serious problems. The Americans chose to simply stonewall the British, with President Roosevelt suggesting the issue could be postponed until Germany's assumed defeat in the summer of 1945.

However, two months after the Cairo Conference, Admiral Sir Percy Noble, stationed in Washington DC, suggested to the US high command the idea of deploying a modern British naval force under General Douglas MacArthur's command in the South-West Pacific theatre. Although the United States Navy (USN) supported MacArthur with the resources of the US Seventh Fleet, the theatre itself was largely outside USN control. Noble suggested a force of two fleet carriers and modernized battlecruiser *Renown* be deployed to the Pacific to operate under US Seventh Fleet. However, the following month the retreating Japanese withdrew major fleet units to Singapore, suspending this possibility.

The British chiefs refused to be stonewalled forever, and in June 1944 they again broached the Far East theatre while meeting with their US counterparts in London. The American chiefs suggested the British reinforce the Indian Ocean area, an area of obvious British interest and a region that would not interfere with the Americans' decisive offensive in the Pacific. A continued secondary option was for British forces to serve under MacArthur in the already multinational South-West Pacific Area, a theatre the US chiefs knew would be a backwater by the time any major British forces appeared. American reluctance to allow the British into the Pacific was more than simple jealousy but was also based on seemingly legitimate factors. US planners believed only final victory mattered, and convinced themselves that:

> Our national interests do not require us to devise operations by US forces which are not directly contributory to our main effort in order to seize areas of post-war strategic importance.
>
> In general, our strategic policy does not require either the exclusion or inclusion of the British, Russians, Dutch or French from participation in the seizure of any enemy-held territory in the Far East. The question of participation in each case should be decided solely on the basis of military consideration from the US point of view.

Secondly, there was a sincere and legitimate belief that the British did not comprehend the staggering distances and logistic planning required for deep Pacific operations, and that when the British inevitably came up short of supplies, the already-strained American logistic system would be stuck bailing them out.

Nonetheless, the issue of final British Far East strategy continued to pick up steam. Just days after Pearl Harbor, in 1941, the British government had extracted an agreement with the United States that the great weight of American strength would concentrate first on defeating Germany before turning against Japan. This was a promise the Americans had largely honoured, and with Germany now clearly en route to total defeat, the British government was anxious to return the favour. Therefore, all British parties agreed that Britain must make a major contribution to defeating Japan as soon as possible. However, even setting aside American intransigence, the first eight months of 1944 were essentially lost, as Churchill and his own chiefs themselves vehemently disagreed on proper British grand strategy in the Far East.

Churchill was at heart a romantic who believed in an anachronistic idea of the British Empire. To Churchill, Britain's proper Far East strategy was to directly reconquer its lost South-East Asia colonies from Japanese forces. As the US chiefs preferred, this implied major naval and amphibious operations on the Indian Ocean littoral, far removed from the main American war in the

Pacific, and generally redundant to it. Churchill even sold this scheme to the approving Americans as pinning down major Japanese forces in Singapore and thus allowing the Americans a 'clear field' in the open Pacific. More importantly, by effecting this strategy Churchill believed he could directly restore British imperial power and prestige to his glittering notions of its pre-war image.

To the British chiefs of staff, however, Churchill's imperialist notions were entirely obsolete, and the strategy Churchill urged was both militarily and politically uneconomic. The chiefs insisted the Indian Ocean region was simply not a decisive theatre and that in any case the British Empire could not be restored to its earlier glory. However, a strong British naval force fighting alongside the main US fleet, in the decisive Pacific theatre, was a more efficient use of military resources and manpower, would more directly contribute to the final defeat of Japan, and would prove much more politically valuable in a post-war world which all but Churchill could see would be dominated by the United States.

For months the impasse dragged on, but by September 1944 Germany suddenly appeared on the verge of collapse. The Allies' Second Quebec Conference ('Octagon'), held that month, duly assumed that Germany would be defeated in October 1944, and thus scheduled the defeat of Japan for October 1945. Although history proved otherwise, in September 1944 events seemed to be racing past the British, and simply forced a decision to be made. At Octagon Churchill caved, and the British government agreed to send a major fleet to the Pacific by December 1944. According to a prominent BPF historian: 'It was quite clear that in the intensive, efficient, and hard striking type of war the US Fleet was fighting, nothing but the inclusion of a big British force would be noticeable and nothing but the best would be tolerated.' The British delegation therefore pledged an eventual four fleet carriers, four light fleet carriers, 14 escort carriers, two battleships, eight cruisers, 24 fleet destroyers and 60 escort vessels.

Substantial British assistance in defeating Japan would obviously be well-received by the American public. As a masterful politician, President Franklin Roosevelt suddenly claimed that the British proposal was 'No sooner offered than accepted.' In fact, Roosevelt's own naval high command remained cool to the idea of a British Pacific Fleet.

Even after the Octagon decision, US Navy chief Ernest J. King's first choice for the Royal Navy was still that it remain in the Indian Ocean and conduct operations in the Bay of Bengal. If King were forced to allow a major British naval force to operate in the Pacific, he preferred that it be in the Netherlands East Indies area, striking at Japanese oil refineries. King also still quietly considered that the British force be put under MacArthur's control in the South-West Pacific theatre (as King's own US Seventh Fleet already was). While both ideas were conceivably useful, they were also outside the main Central Pacific war.

According to the BPF's future carrier commander, Admiral Philip Vian:

Admiral King's attitude has sometimes been ascribed to Anglophobia. This is not altogether true. Certainly the Admiral's loyalty was given wholeheartedly to the Navy he served. It was a feeling which led him to look upon even the United States Army and Air Force as little better than doubtful allies. It was perhaps engendered in some degree by jealousy of the Royal Navy, which had for so long dominated the oceans of the world. Now, when the United States Navy had outstripped our own in size and importance, and was poised to deliver, unaided, decisive defeat on the Japanese Fleet, it was understandable that King should want no one else to share the laurels.

Meanwhile, a converted Churchill stated the intended purpose and mission of the future BPF in a 28 September 1944 report to Parliament:

> The new phase of the war against Japan will command all our resources from the moment the German War is ended. We owe it to Australia and New Zealand to help them remove forever the Japanese menace to their homelands, and as they have helped us on every front in the fight against Germany we will not be behindhand in giving them effective aid. … We have offered the fine modern British fleet and asked that it should be employed in the main operations against Japan. For a year past our modern battleships have been undergoing modification and tropicalization to meet wartime changes in technical apparatus. The scale of our effort will be limited only by the availability of shipping.

However, only in November did a reluctant USN agree, even unofficially, to a British fleet in the Pacific. Accordingly, on 22 November 1944 the traditional Trincomalee, Ceylon-based British Eastern Fleet was divided into two fleets. The first was the East Indies Fleet, which remained based in Ceylon as an Indian Ocean force. The second was the fast carrier-based British Pacific Fleet, which comprised the bulk of the Eastern Fleet's power and would transfer to Australia to fight front-line Japanese forces in the open Pacific alongside the US Pacific Fleet. The British Pacific Fleet's political and strategic mission was complex. Its major objectives can be defined as follows:

1. Ensure that the Americans did not defeat Japan entirely on their own.
2. Restore British political and military prestige east of Suez by avenging 1941–42 defeats.

The crew of Illustrious-class carrier HMS *Formidable* line the deck as they sail into Sydney harbour in 1945. British carriers were designed for a smaller air group than their US counterparts but proved particularly valuable for their more resilient flight decks. (Bettmann/Getty Images)

BRITISH PACIFIC FLEET BASES AND OPERATIONS

3. Indirectly recover lost British colonies by defeating Japan.
4. Reassure Australia and New Zealand of London's dedication and loyalty to the Commonwealth.
5. Learn the revolutionary 'fast carrier' naval strike tactics directly from the Americans while the opportunity still existed.

But perhaps the best explanation was given by Vian: 'There were to be no grounds for critics to say that, having extracted all help she could from the Americans to defeat Hitler, Britain had stood idly by and allowed the Americans to bear the full brunt of the war in the Far East.'

The British Pacific Fleet faced numerous political and logistic hurdles from the Americans, the Commonwealth and its own Admiralty. As stated, many USN officers protested the BPF's inclusion in the Pacific War, worrying that the BPF would be a logistic drain on the already-strained American supply network. (However, the traditional view that the USN protested the BPF mostly on grounds of prestige is not exactly true). Australia's wartime population of 7 million was already in full war economy mode and its government (and labour unions) did not believe Australia could support the influx of 675,000 new British military personnel. Back in London, the Admiralty argued against strategically and tactically subordinating the Royal Navy to the US Pacific Fleet. Additionally, by 1944 the United States was clearly the dominant force in the Allies' war in the Pacific, meaning British high command would always have to consider American political, strategic and logistic sensibilities when making decisions.

As late as December 1944 the BPF's exact arrangement with the USN was still uncertain. The possibility remained that the BPF would be allocated to Vice Admiral Thomas Kinkaid's US Seventh Fleet in MacArthur's South-West Pacific area, rather than accompanying US Pacific commander-in-chief Admiral Nimitz's US fast carriers in the desired Central Pacific theatre. Admiral Fraser and his staff therefore flew to Pearl Harbor to meet their new masters and sound out their intentions. Fraser of course hoped to persuade Nimitz to use the BPF in the decisive theatre. The two good-natured admirals hit it off immediately, and the conference was a great success. Fraser's team returned to Sydney convinced of Nimitz's enthusiasm for deploying the BPF alongside the main US fleet. The only caveat was that Nimitz insisted that Japanese capital ships were 'off limits' to the BPF, in order that the US Pacific Fleet could fully avenge Pearl Harbor on its own. Nevertheless, days after their Hawaii meeting, Nimitz messaged Fraser in Sydney: 'The British force will greatly increase our striking power and demonstrate our unity of purpose against Japan. The United States Pacific Fleet welcomes you.'

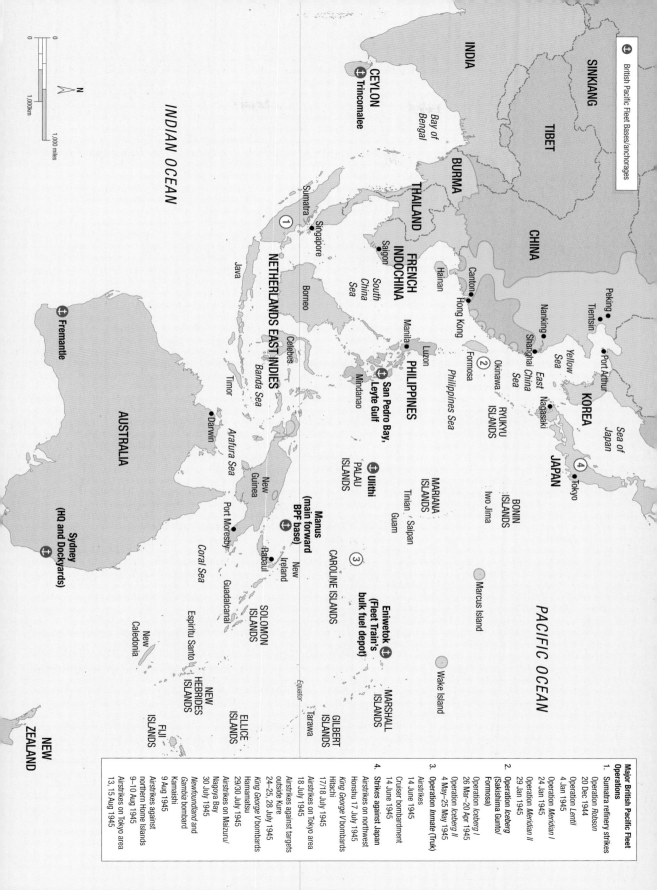

British Pacific Fleet Bases/anchorages

SINKIANG

TIBET

CHINA

INDIA

BURMA

THAILAND

FRENCH INDOCHINA

Bay of Bengal

CEYLON
⊕ Trincomalee

INDIAN OCEAN

Sumatra

Singapore ①

Saigon

South China Sea

Hainan

Canton

Hong Kong

NETHERLANDS EAST INDIES

Java

Borneo

Celebes

Banda Sea

Timor

Nanking

Shanghai

East China Sea

Yellow Sea

Peking

Tientsin

Port Arthur

KOREA

Sea of Japan

Nagasaki

Formosa

② Okinawa

RYUKYU ISLANDS

JAPAN

④ Tokyo

Manila

Luzon

PHILIPPINES

Mindanao

⊕ San Pedro Bay, Leyte Gulf

Philippines Sea

Iwo Jima

BONIN ISLANDS

Marcus Island

PACIFIC OCEAN

Wake Island

⊕ Uitibi

PALAU ISLANDS

Tinian / Saipan

Guam

MARIANA ISLANDS

Darwin

Arafura Sea

New Guinea

Port Moresby

AUSTRALIA

Sydney (HQ and Dockyards) ⊕

Fremantle ⊕

Coral Sea

Rabaul

New Ireland

Manus (main forward BPF base) ⊕

③

CAROLINE ISLANDS

Eniwetok ⊕ (Fleet Train's bulk fuel depot)

Equator

MARSHALL ISLANDS

Guadalcanal

SOLOMON ISLANDS

New Caledonia

Espiritu Santo

NEW HEBRIDES ISLANDS

ELLICE ISLANDS

Tarawa

GILBERT ISLANDS

FIJI ISLANDS

NEW ZEALAND

N

0
1,000km

0
1,000 miles

Major British Pacific Fleet Operations

1. Sumatra refinery strikes
   Operation *Robson*
   20 Dec 1944
   Operation *Lentil*
   4 Jan 1945
   Operation *Meridian I*
   24 Jan 1945
   Operation *Meridian II*
   29 Jan 1945

2. Operation *Iceberg*
   (Sakishima Gunto/
   Formosa)
   Operation *Iceberg I*
   26 Mar–20 Apr 1945
   Operation *Iceberg II*
   4 May–25 May 1945

3. Operation *Inmate* (Truk)
   Airstrikes
   14 June 1945
   Cruiser bombardment
   14 June 1945

4. Strikes against Japan
   Airstrikes on northwest
   Honshu 17 July 1945
   King George V bombards
   Hitachi
   17/18 July 1945
   Airstrikes on Tokyo area
   18 July 1945
   Airstrikes against targets
   outside Kure
   24–25, 28 July 1945
   King George V bombards
   Hamamatsu
   29/30 July 1945
   Airstrikes on Maizuru/
   Nagoya Bay
   30 July 1945
   Newfoundland and
   Gambia bombard
   Kamaishi
   9 Aug 1945
   Airstrikes against
   northern Home Islands
   9–10 Aug 1945
   Airstrikes on Tokyo area
   13, 15 Aug 1945

FLEET FIGHTING POWER

THE SHIPS

By 1942 the Admiralty acknowledged that the aircraft carrier had superseded the battleship as the Royal Navy's primary striking weapon. Future Royal Navy battle fleets would be built around the aircraft carrier and its aircraft. Fast battleships and cruisers would directly support the carriers by providing anti-surface and anti-air defence, while flotillas of ever-versatile destroyers would function as the force's outer screen, maintaining their traditional missions as multi-purpose escorts and anti-submarine warfare specialists.

With the Atlantic war winding down in 1944–45, the BPF received the most modern Royal Navy warships and equipment available. The BPF's grand total came to six fleet carriers, four light carriers, two aircraft maintenance carriers, nine escort carriers, over 750 aircraft, four fast battleships, 11 cruisers, 35 destroyers, 14 frigates, 44 corvettes, sloops and smaller warships, 31 submarines and 54 large ships in the Fleet Train.

The BPF's primary striking power resided in the six Illustrious- and Implacable-class armoured fleet carriers (no more than four were ever deployed simultaneously). Alongside them were several King George V-class battleships (no more than two simultaneously). Leander-, Dido-, Bellona-, Fiji- and Minotaur-class light cruisers were employed in the anti-aircraft screen. Several late-war classes of British destroyers served in the anti-aircraft and anti-submarine warfare roles.

Over the course of 1944, powerful Royal Navy units began to slowly trickle back into the eastern Indian Ocean. Fleet carrier *Illustrious* arrived at Trincomalee on 28 January 1944, accompanied by maintenance aircraft carrier *Unicorn*. They were joined at Ceylon by fleet carriers *Victorious* and *Indomitable* in July, battleship *Howe* in August, and carrier *Indefatigable* and battleship *King George V* in December.

Much has been made of British ships being unsuited for tropical environments. This is true; British ships were badly ventilated, not air conditioned, and throughout the day their poorly insulated steel hulls soaked up the tropical heat and sunshine, inspiring many crew to sleep on deck at night whenever possible. What is rarely mentioned is that all these facts were also true of American ships. However, there was one important difference when it came to carriers. US carriers had wooden flight decks and their hangars were open, which likely made American hangar decks more comfortable to work in than their British counterparts.

Fleet Carriers

The 1936 building programme allowed two new 23,000-ton carriers. Three geared turbines would deliver 111,000shp to three shafts, driving the new Illustrious class to a top speed of 30.5 knots. Endurance would be 10,700nm at 10 knots. In contrast to the wooden-decked *Ark Royal*, laid down in 1935, the Illustrious class was designed around an armoured box extending most of the length of the ship. The box's top was the flight deck, built out of 3in-thick armour plating designed to resist a direct hit from a 500lb bomb. The sides and fore-and-aft bulkheads comprised 4.5in armour. However, such weight high in the ship constrained *Illustrious* to a single hangar, meaning a total of only 36 planes could be carried compared to *Ark Royal*'s 60. Nevertheless, by installing outriggers extending from the flight deck, an American-style deck park system would eventually be adopted that raised aircraft capacity to 56 planes.

Carrier HMS *Indomitable* viewed from above during Pacific service. Sixteen Chance-Vought Corsairs and nine Fairey Fireflies can be seen crowding the armoured flight deck. *Indomitable* is employing the recently adopted deck park system. (IWM A 29080)

The original anti-aircraft battery comprised 16 QF (quick-firing) 4.5in DP (dual-purpose) guns in twin mounts and six octuple QF 2-pdr guns, although by 1945 the carriers had mounted additional batteries of Bofors 40mm and Oerlikon 20mm guns.

The lead ship *Illustrious* entered service in summer 1940, followed by *Formidable* in October 1940. The third and fourth Illustrious-class carriers, *Victorious* and *Indomitable*, would be of modified designs. Both would employ a slightly longer hull accommodating an enlarged powerplant. Additionally, late modifications to *Indomitable* reduced the side armour to just 1.5 inches (3.8cm), raised the flight deck by 14ft (4.2m) and squeezed two lower-ceilinged hangars into the hull instead of the original one-storey hangar. This allowed *Indomitable* a design complement of 45 planes instead of 36. *Victorious* would enter service in April 1941, and *Indomitable* would follow in December 1941.

The next two fleet carriers, *Implacable* and *Indefatigable*, were classified separately as the Implacable-class. When compared to the Illustrious-class, the Implacables were given a fourth geared steam turbine, raising power output to 148,000shp and increasing top speed to 32.5 knots. Range was 12,000nm at 10 knots. To keep the Implacables within the same 23,000-ton limit as the Illustrious-class, the Implacables' hangar decks and hangar bulkhead armour were thinned.

One major improvement to the Implacable class was the planned use of an American-style deck park, which allowed these carriers to eventually carry 81 aircraft each. However, a major issue with the Illustrious and Implacable classes was their low hangars, which were variously 14ft (4.2m) and 16ft (4.8m) high; the BPF's American-built aircraft were designed for 17ft (5.1m) hangars.

The Implacables mounted 16 QF 4.5in DP guns in eight twin turrets, plus five octuple and one quadruple QF 2-pdr batteries, plus about 60 Oerlikon 20mm autocannons, although many of the Oerlikons were replaced by more powerful Bofors 40mm guns for Pacific service.

Both *Implacable* and *Indefatigable* entered service in summer 1944. All six Illustrious- and Implacable-class fleet carriers would ultimately serve in the Pacific, where they were assigned to the 1st Aircraft Carrier Squadron (1 ACS), which formed the heart of the BPF's strike force. All would see action with the 1 ACS, although never more than four at once.

Light Carriers

In 1942 the Admiralty had commenced a crash carrier-building programme that eventually resulted in 16 light carriers of the nearly identical Colossus and Majestic classes. These carriers displaced only 13,200 tons, being small, unarmoured, and designed for mass production. Unlike the USN's Independence-class light carriers, the British light carriers were not true fast carriers as they could only make 25 knots. However, unlike previous British carriers, they were fitted with air conditioning. The class's designed air group was 37 planes, increased to 48 with a deck park.

The lead ship, *Colossus*, was commissioned in December 1944. *Colossus*, *Glory*, *Venerable* and *Vengeance* were earmarked for the BPF, where they were

Battleship HMS *Howe* at Auckland, January 1945. Howe was visiting New Zealand as Fraser's British Pacific Fleet flagship. Political and administrative realities would force Fraser to relinquish at-sea control to his deputy commander Rawlings. (HMSO/Public Domain)

scheduled to form the BPF's second carrier formation, 11th Aircraft Carrier Squadron (11 ACS). All were en route to the Pacific in summer 1945, but just missed hostilities by a matter of days. They would help serve in the liberation and occupation phase that immediately followed the ceasefire.

Battleships

The BPF was designed to be the fastest, most modern striking force the Royal Navy could put to sea in 1945. Combined with Britain's severe manpower shortage, this meant only the modern, war-built King George V-class fast battleships would see action in the open Pacific.

The King George V-class design had been limited to 14in guns by the London Naval Treaty of March 1936. However, within months the treaty began to fall apart, but the King George V scheme was too far along to be modified. This meant the King George V class was the only modern fast battleship with 14in guns, but the design did carry ten 14in guns in two quadruple turrets and one twin turret, instead of the usual eight or nine heavier guns carried by other navies. Secondary armament comprised 16 5.25in DP guns in eight twin turrets. By 1945 *King George V* boasted a powerful anti-aircraft battery of 64 2-pdr pom-poms, eight Bofors 40mm cannon and 37 Oerlikon 20mm guns.

Standard displacement was 36,727 tons, allowing protection designed to resist 15in shells. The King George V class performed well in several duels with German battleships, but by 1945 the chance of encountering an operational

VICTORIOUS HIT BY A KAMIKAZE, 1 APRIL 1945 (overleaf)

The afternoon of 1 April 1945 saw Task Force 57 cruising beneath patchy 500ft cloud cover. Then at 1735hrs a Zero carrying a 550lb bomb suddenly burst from the low-hanging clouds towards *Victorious*. Erupting with anti-aircraft fire, *Victorious* now turned violently. The pursuing Zero, trying to follow *Victorious*, curved towards the stern and almost seemed to struggle to keep up with the carrier's manoeuvre. *Victorious*'s Captain Denny would later state:

'*Victorious* was now swinging very fast and as we watched the aircraft banked more steeply trying to keep on the target. He roared in and his starboard wing struck the port edge of the flight deck and caused his plane to cartwheel into the sea on the port side. The bomb detonated underwater about 80ft clear of the ship's side and threw tons of water, a quantity of petrol and many fragments of the aircraft and pilot on to the flight deck.'

According to eyewitnesses aboard nearby *King George V*, it was impossible to tell whether *Victorious* had been hit or had been near-missed. The plane seemed to have hit the carrier's flight deck and:

> '... her bow disappeared for about 30 seconds in a ball of black smoke, flying chunks of debris and an immense column of water ... our concern subsided as she reappeared and we received the report that her only damage consisted of a few bow plates that were strained by the force of the explosion.'

Although TF-57's armoured carriers suffered considerably more damage from Japanese air attack than prevailing myth allows, none suffered any catastrophic episode like that which befell several of their American counterparts. Nor were any TF-57 ships ever threatened with sinking, compared to the scores of US destroyers, auxiliaries and landing ships that were sunk off Okinawa by Japanese action.

BOMBARDING HAMAMATSU, 29/30 JULY 1945

At 1100hrs on 29 July, Rear Admiral Shafroth's Bombardment Group Able (TU-34.8.1) of three fast battleships, four heavy cruisers and ten destroyers detached from TF-38 to shell Hamamatsu, a manufacturing city of 162,000 inhabitants.

TU-34.8.1 fell into column and was joined by the British TU-37.1.2, comprising Rawlings' flagship, battleship *King George V*, plus destroyers *Undine*, *Ulysses* and *Urania*. TU-37.1.2 now fell into the rear of the combined column. All warships in the entire formation, regardless of type or nationality, were separated from their immediate neighbours by 1,000 yards to the front or back and 1,250 yards abeam.

Radar contact was established with Honshu at a range of 63nm. The combined force commenced a high-speed approach to the target at 2203hrs. The initial approach was roughly east to west. The battleships opened fire at 2321hrs on 29 July. A total of two bombardment runs were made, allowing the bombardment force to make a single 180-degree course reversal so that their second run would be outbound. At 0027hrs on 30 July, the bombardment groups ceased firing and retired to the east.

Canadian Fiji-class light cruiser HMCS *Uganda* seen in 1945. *Uganda* was Canada's most prominent contribution to the British Pacific Fleet, and the only front-line warship. Transferred to the Royal Canadian Navy on Trafalgar Day 1944, *Uganda* would achieve considerable notoriety when two-thirds of the crew voted to legally leave the Pacific War. (IWM ABS 698)

Japanese battleship was virtually zero. However, *King George V* and *Howe* would get multiple opportunities to exercise their heavy batteries against shore targets – first against the Sakashima Gunto airfields in May 1945, and then against Home Islands industrial targets in July. Like the American fast battleships operating with the US carrier force, the King George V class's primary contribution to the BPF was the powerful defensive umbrella they provided the carriers with from their heavy anti-aircraft batteries. The King George Vs had a nominal top speed of 28 knots, but their actual operational speed proved to be 1–2 knots less, slowing the carrier force.

Five King George V-class battleships were completed in total, but only two – *King George V* and *Howe* – saw combat with the BPF. Both battleships bombarded Sakashima airfields during *Iceberg*, while *King George V* twice bombarded mainland Japan. *King George V* entered service in late 1940, followed by *Prince of Wales* in spring 1941. *Prince of Wales*, however, was sunk by Japanese bombers in December 1941 defending Malaya. The third vessel, *Howe*, entered service in summer 1942. The two remaining King George V-class battleships, *Duke of York* and *Anson*, were assigned to the BPF and were en route to the Pacific when the war ended.

Light Cruisers

Several classes of light cruiser served in the medium combatant role, always with the carrier strike force.

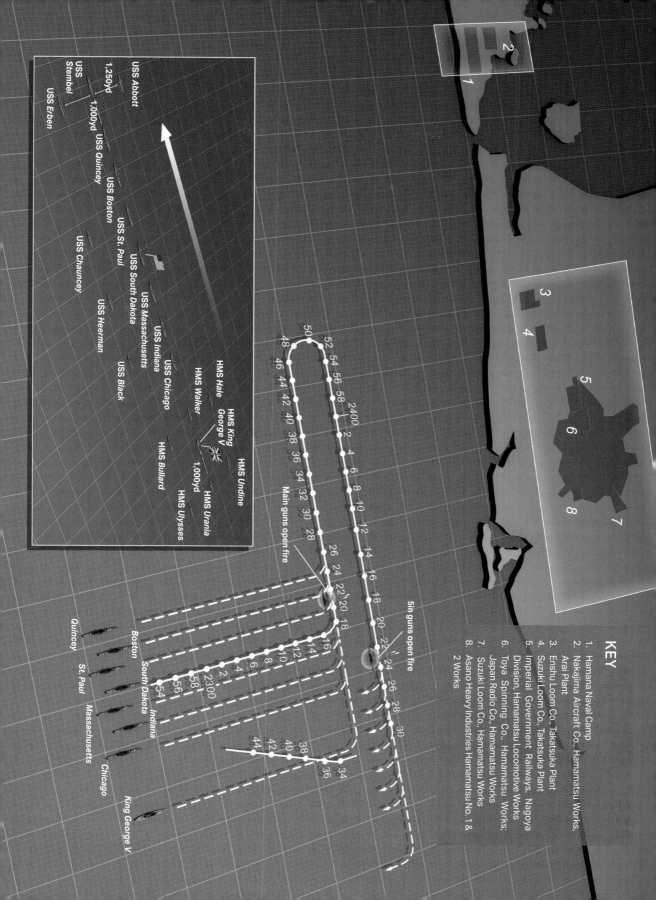

KEY

1. Hamana Naval Camp
2. Nakajima Aircraft Co., Hamamatsu Works, Arai Plant
3. Enshu Loom Co., Takatsuka Plant
4. Suzuki Loom Co., Takatsuka Plant
5. Imperial Government Railways, Nagoya Division, Hamamatsu Locomotive Works
6. Toya Spinning Co., Hamamatsu Works; Japan Radio Co., Hamamatsu Works;
7. Suzuki Loom Co., Hamamatsu Works
8. Asano Heavy Industries Hamamatsu No. 1 & 2 Works

USS Erben
USS Stembel
1,000yd USS Quincey
1,250yd
USS Abbott
USS Boston
USS St. Paul
USS South Dakota
USS Chauncey
USS Massachusetts
USS Indiana
USS Heerman
USS Chicago
HMS Walker
HMS Hale
HMS King George V
HMS Bullard
1,000yd
HMS Urania
HMS Ulysses
HMS Undine

Main guns open fire
5in guns open fire

2400
2300

Quincey
Boston
South Dakota
Indiana
St. Paul
Massachusetts
Chicago
King George V

They functioned as anti-aircraft defence for the carriers, and occasionally bombarded shore targets. Standard top speed for all BPF light cruisers was 32 knots.

The first Leander-class light cruisers were commissioned in 1933. Displacing 7,270 tons, they made 32.5 knots on 72,000shp. Intended for the commerce protection role, the Leanders were armed with eight 6in/50 Mk XXIII guns in twin mounts, four 4in Mk V guns in single mounts, and three quad .50-calibre machine guns. Of eight Leanders completed, only HMNZS *Achilles* served in the BPF. By 1945 *Achilles* had seen one of the 6in/50 twin mounts removed and replaced by 40mm and 20mm anti-aircraft guns.

In 1940 the Royal Navy commissioned the first of an eventual 16 Dido-class light cruisers. Displacing 5,600 tons, they were intended as small trade protection cruisers. The Didos' standard fit comprised ten 5.25in/50 Mk I guns in five twin mounts, two quadruple 2-pdr pom-poms, and two quad .50-calibre machine guns. Three cruisers of this class – HMS *Argonaut*, HMS *Euryalus* and HMS *Black Prince* – saw action with the BPF.

In 1940 the Royal Navy began commissioning the first of 11 Fiji-class (or Crown Colony-class) light cruisers. Displacing 8,530 tons, the Fijis mounted nine to 12 6in/50 Mk XXIII guns in triple mounts, eight 4in Mk XVI guns in four twin mounts, two to three quadruple 2-pdr pom-poms, and 16 to 20 Oerlikon 20mm guns in single or twin mounts. Ultimately serving with the BPF were HMNZS *Gambia*, HMS *Newfoundland* and HMCS *Uganda*.

A single Minotaur-class light cruiser, HMS *Swiftsure*, would see action with the BPF. At 8,800 tons, *Swiftsure* mounted nine 6in/50 Mk XXIII guns in three triple mounts, ten 4in Mk XVI guns in five twin mounts, four quadruple 2-pdr pom-poms, two quad .50-calibre machine guns, and twenty-two 20mm guns. Although HMS *Swiftsure* was the last Royal Navy cruiser completed in the war, this was the first light cruiser designed around a new, more efficient operations room. *Swiftsure* was the BPF's most efficient cruiser against enemy aircraft.

Q-class destroyer HMS *Quadrant* steams alongside carrier USS *Wasp* off Japan, July 1945. The Q-class comprised the 3rd Emergency Flotilla of wartime destroyer construction. HMS *Quadrant* was transferred to the Royal Australian Navy in October 1945. (Public Domain)

Destroyers

BPF destroyers were largely used to provide an anti-aircraft and anti-submarine screen for TF-57/TF-37, although some also escorted Fleet Train convoys. They also functioned as forward radar pickets. The BPF's destroyers were drawn from the N, Q, T, U and W classes. Medium and light anti-aircraft batteries differed slightly among classes and ships. A typical example might be a quadruple 2-pdr pom-pom and eight Oerlikon 20mm guns, with many mounts replaced by Bofors 40mm by 1945. The top speed of the destroyers was about 36 knots.

Displacing 1,690 tons, by 1945 the N class carried six 4.7in guns in three twin turrets, one 4in AA gun aft, five 21in torpedo tubes, and 45 depth charges. The similar Q, T, U and W classes displaced about 1,710 tons and mounted four single QF 4.7in guns, plus eight (T, U and W classes) or ten (Q-class) 21in torpedo tubes, and up to 45 depth charges.

A single Battle-class destroyer, HMS *Barfleur*, was commissioned in time to see action with the BPF. *Barfleur* displaced 2,315 tons and mounted four 4.5in guns, one 4in AA gun, four twin Bofors 40mm guns, two twin and two single Oerlikon 20mm guns, and eight 21in torpedo tubes.

Submarines

The Royal Navy's 2nd and 8th Submarine Flotillas were transferred from the East Indies Fleet to the BPF on 1 April 1945 and operated out of Subic Bay in the Philippines. They were supported by the submarine depot ships *Adamant* and *Maidstone* respectively. The 2nd and 8th Flotillas comprised mostly S- and T-class submarines. The S-class displaced 840 tons and had a top speed of nearly 15 knots surfaced and 8 knots submerged. Six 21in torpedo tubes were mounted forward and one aft. Deck guns comprised a QF 4in gun, a 20mm cannon and three .303-calibre machine guns.

Displacing 1,290 tons, the superior T-class was faster at 15.5 knots surfaced and 9 knots submerged. In addition to a QF 4in deck gun, six bow and four external 21in torpedo tubes were fitted. Loadout was 16 Mark VIII torpedoes. Designed with the Pacific in mind, the T-class had an 8,000nm range at 10 knots.

XE Craft

The BPF also deployed a class of 33-ton midget submarine. This so-called XE craft had a four-man crew, including a trained diver. A pair of 4,000lb Minol charges could be carried by each XE craft. Additionally, an airlock allowed the diver to sortie from a submerged XE craft and manually attach limpet mines below the target's waterline. Six XE craft, supported by the specialized depot ship HMS *Bonaventure*, deployed with the BPF as the 14th Submarine Flotilla.

TECHNICAL FACTORS

By late 1944/early 1945 the Royal Navy could afford to send its best ships to the Pacific. However, even the best British ships, aircraft and equipment were short-range, pre-war designs intended to operate in the North Atlantic and the Mediterranean. Strike forces composed of capital ships had expected to make relatively short, round-trip operational excursions from the pre-war Royal Navy's vast, worldwide network of friendly bases. Instead, by 1945 British naval forces were being forced to operate at extreme long ranges and at high operational tempos deep in the Pacific Ocean. For decades USN equipment and doctrine had been designed to operate in this unique theatre. Their British counterparts had not, and yet they would be operating alongside the Americans and according to American concepts.

To briefly illustrate the problem, consider that the BPF's main weapon, its Illustrious-class fleet carriers, had a cruising range of 10,700nm at 10 knots. Their USN counterparts, the Essex-class carriers, had an endurance of 20,000nm at 15 knots. In short, the Royal Navy was forced to operate well outside its comfort zone. The BPF's story, therefore, is often one of remarkable adaptation and inspired improvisation.

Personnel

Although all carriers and battleships belonged to the Royal Navy, a handful of cruisers, destroyers and smaller escorts were provided by the Royal Canadian Navy, the Royal New Zealand Navy and the Royal Australian Navy. Additionally, many Commonwealth sailors served aboard Royal Navy ships, ensuring a cross-section of the Commonwealth was well represented in the BPF. Indeed, in 1945 the BPF's Fleet Air Arm contingent was 25 per cent New Zealander, with other Dominions also heavily represented. Many BPF airmen were RAF transfers.

British warships were essentially designed for week-long excursions, whereas American doctrine expected months in between true port calls. Unsurprisingly British ships were not as liveable as their American counterparts, whose doctrine demanded extreme long range and whose ship designs necessarily emphasized habitability. A US liaison officer suggested that BPF aircrew were more prone to battle fatigue because of the relative 'lack of necessities, conveniences and comforts' aboard British carriers. Among other issues, British sailors slept in hammocks rather than bunks, they had less personal living space and their rations were generally not as fresh or as prolific (most famously, British ships lacked the Americans' ice cream machines). Meals were served 19th-century style in individual messes rather than the USN's more modern cafeteria-style halls. However, British sailors could drink alcohol aboard, a practice strictly outlawed in the USN. Additionally, most BPF escort carriers were American-built, with American-style accommodation.

Carrier Aircraft

Alone among the pre-war powers, the Royal Navy had fully expected to operate in every ocean in the world. However, by the early 1930s the Royal Navy assumed its next naval war would be against a rising and expansionist Japan. Its next carrier, *Ark Royal*, had a wooden flight deck and was designed for 72 aircraft to fight in the open waters of the Pacific. However, by 1936 the rapidly increasing power and aggression of Nazi Germany and Fascist Italy led to a refocus on Europe. Subsequent British carriers were therefore designed for constricted European and Mediterranean waters, where they were expected to fall under land-based bomber attack. The Royal Navy's new focus was on carrier survivability, which meant heavily armoured flight decks. Unlike the Americans, the Royal Navy also emphasized protecting its aircraft from both weather and enemy attack by stowing all aircraft below in armoured hangars. All this contributed to new British carrier designs that were considerably better protected than US carriers, albeit wielding significantly smaller air groups than their American counterparts, which emphasized air group size and massed striking power above all else.

Political fallout stretching back decades meant the BPF employed many different types of carrier aircraft. Although the Supermarine Seafire and Fairey Firefly were British designs, roughly 76 per cent of the carrier planes embarked by BPF carriers were American models, specifically the Grumman Hellcat and Chance-Vought Corsair fighters, and the Grumman Avenger torpedo bomber. These American types were designed specifically to operate from carriers and naturally performed better under the circumstances. However, the American-built aircraft had been so modified to Fleet Air Arm standards that little of their equipment remained interchangeable with American parts.

The Supermarine Seafire was a navalized Spitfire. First operating from Royal Navy carriers in late 1942, the Seafire was a superb fighter, with excellent agility and climb performance. Its 1,585hp Rolls-Royce Merlin 55M engine gave the Seafire F Mk III a top speed of 400mph. However, because it was based on a ground-based interceptor, the Seafire suffered from terribly short fuel endurance, while its narrow, flimsy landing gear proved extremely dangerous in carrier operations, causing many fatal accidents. Compared to the Hellcat and Corsair, Seafires averaged fewer sorties per day and their cripplingly short radius limited them to Fleet Combat Air Patrol (CAP) missions only. Yet even when flying CAP missions their endurance aloft was so short that the carriers were constantly required to manoeuvre into the wind to replace shifts, frustrating the fleet's operational navigation. Such operational limitations inspired Fraser to describe the Seafire as 'triply inferior to Hellcats and Corsairs'. However, by July 1945 90-gallon drop tanks would help increase the Seafire's operational range, finally allowing it to fly offensive sweeps against the Home Islands.

In early 1943 the Lend-Lease programme had begun providing the United States' most advanced carrier aircraft to the Fleet Air Arm. These were purpose-designed carrier aircraft that had been developed in a far healthier political environment for naval aviation than the pre-war Royal Navy had been allowed. Unsurprisingly, the American aircraft were categorically superior for carrier operations than their British-designed counterparts. After the early 1945 raids on Sumatra, Vian reported the BPF's pleasure at the American-type carrier aircraft it employed – the Avengers, Corsairs and Hellcats. The American planes' 'robustness, reliability and long endurance showed up in marked contrast to our own types'.

The Grumman Hellcat F Mk II (F6F-5) was a single-seat fighter/fighter-bomber. It was powered by a Pratt & Whitney R-2800-10W Double Wasp radial engine rated at 2,200hp. This allowed great performance out of the Hellcat, which was unusually large for a single-seat, single-engine fighter. Top speed was 392mph. The Hellcat was particularly rugged, reliable and easy to fly. Ample firepower was provided by six wing-mounted .50-calibre machine guns. Hardpoints allowed two 1,000lb or 500lb bombs, or six 60lb rockets, or two 100-gallon drop tanks to increase range. The first Hellcat F Mk II models began arriving with the Fleet Air Arm in May 1944. A few Hellcats were modified specifically for the photoreconnaissance mission.

The Chance-Vought Corsair Mk II (F4U-1A) was the premier carrier-based fighter-bomber of the war. The Corsair was powered by the 2,000hp R-2800-8 Double Wasp, virtually the same engine as the Hellcat. However, the Corsair's sleeker airframe allowed it a higher top speed of 425mph. With its power and stability in a dive, the Corsair was also an excellent dive-bomber. However, the Corsair handled less forgivingly than the Hellcat, especially on landing.

The Fairey Firefly was a two-seat fighter/strike/reconnaissance aircraft. Its Rolls-Royce Griffon XII engine gave it a top speed of 345mph, and four 20mm wing-mounted cannon imparted plenty of strafing firepower. It could carry two 1,000lb bombs or eight 60lb rockets.

Crewmen load a 21in torpedo aboard a British Pacific Fleet Avenger at a Ceylon airfield, January 1945. At this point in the Pacific War it was a rare chance indeed to drop an aerial torpedo in anger. (Popperfoto via Getty Images)

The BPF's primary bomber was the three-man Grumman Avenger, whose 1,850hp Wright GR-2600-8 Cyclone engine gave the big aircraft a 285mph top speed. A dorsal, turret-mounted .50-calibre machine gun and a ventral .30-calibre machine gun provided trainable defensive weaponry. The Avenger could carry two 1,000lb bombs, four 500lb bombs or eight 60lb rockets.

The Firefly and Avenger were capable strike aircraft, while the Seafire, Hellcat and Corsair were all superior in performance to any Japanese fighters they were likely to face. More importantly, by 1944–45 their pilots, although often inexperienced, were much better trained.

Aboard *Victorious* were two Supermarine Walrus amphibious planes. The ungainly Walrus had a top speed of just 135mph but proved invaluable in the air-sea rescue and utility roles.

By early 1945, British Pacific Fleet aircraft would have their standard Royal Navy markings overhauled to resemble US markings more conspicuously. To avoid friendly fire, all red was removed. Most distinctively, the BPF received its own unique blue-and-white roundel, which intentionally resembled the US roundel's 'circle and bar' shape, while retaining the white ball inside a larger blue circle that was still recognizably British. BPF aircraft also adopted the American style of assigning each carrier a letter, which would then be painted on the tail of each plane assigned to that carrier.

Working with US Carriers, 1943–44

The Royal Navy already had experience working alongside US fast carriers. Between 17 May and 31 July 1943, the Admiralty had temporarily loaned carrier HMS *Victorious* to Halsey's Third Fleet in the South Pacific. *Victorious* served alongside the older US fast carrier *Saratoga*. During this period US oilers repeatedly refuelled *Victorious* at sea, allowing the carrier to stay at sea 28 consecutive days, a new record for a British carrier. *Victorious* steamed 12,223nm in one month, compared to the carrier's previous average of 4,905nm.

In late 1943, carrier USS *Ranger* operated out of Scapa Flow under Home Fleet command. Escorted by British forces, *Ranger* struck Norway in October, but *Ranger*'s captain complained afterwards that the British 'know less of the proper use of carrier air power than we did when the *Langley* was our only carrier' – that is, the 1920s.

Between 27 March and 18 May 1944, Nimitz would loan fast carrier USS *Saratoga* and three escorting destroyers to the Royal Navy's Eastern Fleet. Operating in the Indian Ocean, *Saratoga* and *Illustrious* combined for a successful two-carrier strike against Sabang (Operation *Cockpit*) on 19 April. No mission better illustrates the increasingly multinational make-up of the Far East naval war. Somerville's force included British carrier *Illustrious*, American carrier *Saratoga*, British battleships *Queen Elizabeth* and *Valiant*, French battleship *Richelieu*, British battlecruiser *Renown*, four British cruisers, one New Zealand

AIR TACTICS: TF-57'S CAP ON 12 APRIL 1945

Task Force 57's Fleet CAP usually consisted of four CAP stations, which were defined by altitude relative to each other – their exact altitude could vary from day to day based on conditions. Typically, during daylight hours each station would be patrolled by a four-fighter section, for a total of 16 fighters.

The first three stations were High, Medium and Low-level CAPs, which orbited 10nm-wide circles stacked directly overhead the task force until a threat was identified. The fourth CAP station was the so-called 'Jack' patrol CAP that had only just been invented by the Americans five months earlier to counter extremely low-level attackers. The Jack patrol comprised two sections of two fighters each, which would fan out in separate quadrants where extremely low-level enemy threats were most expected. The Jack patrols would fly near sea-level and within ten miles of the destroyer screen to remain under visual fighter director control.

When possible, Task Force 57 preferred to match the best performing fighter type to each CAP station. This typically meant Corsairs at high altitude, Seafire F Mk IIIs at medium altitude, and Seafire L Mk IIIs at lower altitude.

On 16 April 1945, Task Force 57's CAP tactics were slightly adjusted, both to conserve the fragile Seafires and also to maximize the Hellcats and Corsairs flying offensive CAPs over enemy airfields. At dawn, a small number of Hellcats and Corsairs would be launched to the High CAP position to make long-range interceptions. Fireflies took over the standing Jack patrols, and eight Seafires were held aboard *Indefatigable* ready to scramble if necessary. After three hours the eight standby Seafires would be launched and take over the High CAP and Jack patrol duties and would be replaced on immediate standby by a new force of eight Seafires. After 1200hrs, the numbers would be reduced to four Seafires each airborne and on standby.

cruiser, one Dutch cruiser, and eight British, one Dutch, three Australian and three American destroyers.

However, *Saratoga*'s air group commander, Commander Joe Clifton, was horrified that it took *Illustrious* an hour and a half to launch and rendezvous a single deck-load of planes. Retraining the British air group in American methods, Clifton soon had that time down to 25 minutes.

A second combined strike, Operation *Transom*, was made on 17 May when *Illustrious* and *Saratoga* raided the oil refinery at Surabaya, Java. A single *Saratoga* Avenger was lost. *Saratoga* then departed for the US fleet.

In addition to deck-load strike coordination, the Royal Navy learned additional valuable lessons operating alongside the Americans in 1943 and 1944. Among these were:

1. At least two strikes should always be planned against any target, as the second strike often brought increasing returns.
2. Photoreconnaissance should be made concurrently with an airstrike, and
3. the photographs immediately developed and automatically delivered to the fleet commander (by air drop if need be) before retiring the fleet from the strike zone.
4. Returning strike commanders should likewise be immediately debriefed and their opinions given significant weight before retiring from the strike zone.
5. Flight deck handling crew should be more carefully and efficiently organized along American lines.

Generally, however, the most valuable advantage British carrier personnel gained was developing experience in American-style multi-carrier strike operations.

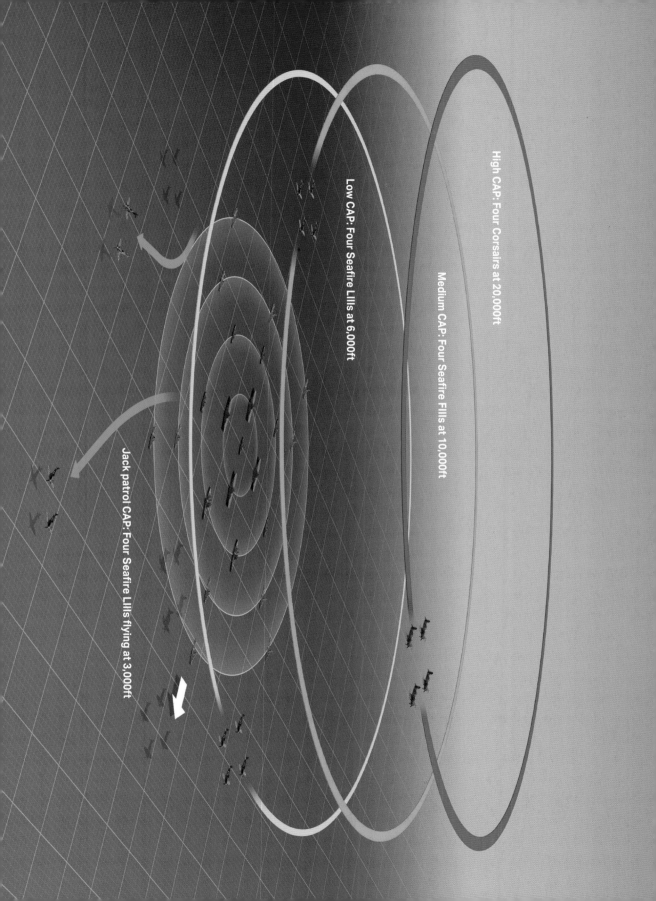

High CAP: Four Corsairs at 20,000ft

Medium CAP: Four Seafire FIIIs at 10,000ft

Low CAP: Four Seafire LIIIs at 6,000ft

Jack patrol CAP: Four Seafire LIIIs flying at 3,000ft

HOW THE FLEET OPERATED

DOCTRINE AND COMMAND
Command

To fully appreciate the BPF's performance, it is necessary to provide a wider view of the Pacific War and the US Pacific Fleet. At the 1941–42 Arcadia conference, the Anglo-American high command, called the Combined Chiefs of Staff (CCS), had formally divided global responsibilities into specific geographical theatres of operations, each under a nominal 'combined' Anglo-American command. The Pacific Ocean was divided into four theatres: a Pacific Ocean Area combining three theatres (North, Central and South Pacific) and a South-West Pacific Area comprising Australia, the Philippines, the East Indies minus Sumatra, and part of the Solomons Islands. In late 1943 the CCS established a further combined Allied command in the Indian Ocean/South East Asia region, called the South East Asia Command (SEAC).

The US Pacific Fleet was divided into several numbered fleets. The Pacific Fleet's main battle fleet and invasion force operated in the Central Pacific. Because its command rotated on a regular schedule, it was known as Fifth Fleet when under the command of Admiral Raymond Spruance, and Third Fleet when under Admiral Bill Halsey. Each admiral had his own staff which rotated with him, but the men, ships and formations remained the same.

In early 1941 the USN had adopted the 'Task Force' concept, whereby a force of any necessary size and configuration would be temporarily assembled for a mission under the command of at least a rear admiral. The task force would receive a two-digit designation based on the US fleet it was assigned to, i.e. Task Force 58 was the powerful US Fast Carrier Task Force, assigned to Fifth Fleet. Task forces could be subdivided as needed into additional task forces or smaller task groups, which were divisible into task units. Each smaller unit's designation derived from adding a decimalization to the designation of the larger unit. This widely flexible format was adopted by the BPF upon its 1944 establishment.

Unlike USN officers, who usually rotated between sea and shore billets, the Royal Navy's combat admirals and captains spent most of the war at sea commands. However, the BPF's assigned commander, Admiral Sir Bruce Fraser, outranked almost all US admirals at sea in the Pacific. Against Royal Navy tradition, Fraser was compelled to remain ashore at Sydney, partially to avoid awkward command situations with the Americans. However, this 'command from the rear' shore-based management mimicked the USN's proven Pacific command style. Considering the enormous theatre-wide responsibilities Fraser faced on land and sea, the decision to command from Sydney was probably correct. The sheer scale, extreme range and unrelenting intensity of the modern Pacific naval war had simply moved past the heroic Nelsonian tradition. Significantly, it was Fraser who insisted (over much Admiralty resistance) that the BPF adopt as many of the USN's operational methods as possible. Under Fraser's direction, the BPF adopted the USN's comprehensive fleet tactical manual, which had been completely overhauled in 1943.

The BPF's fast carrier task force (TF-57/TF-37) was organized overwhelmingly along American lines as much as possible, including using American signalling and formations – US liaison officers and signalling teams were assigned specifically to facilitate this adjustment. There was some ambiguity as to the US officers' authority – were the Americans riding with the BPF there to suggest, direct or order? Veteran British admirals such as Vian naturally considered the Americans there to suggest only.

The December 1944 conference between Fraser and Nimitz had determined that the BPF's main carrier strike force would initially operate separately from the US carrier groups, which would be more efficient than full integration. Operationally the BPF would coordinate with US Fifth Fleet, commanded by Admiral Raymond Spruance. Instead of direct orders, Spruance would give carefully worded 'requests' which the BPF was technically free to refuse.

An unexpected culture shock was the Americans' sheer passion for paperwork. According to *Victorious*'s captain:

Serial orders issued by the numerous British authorities, the American manuals, the operations orders, the intelligence material all relevant to the operation, reports and returns due, when piled on my sea-cabin desk reached to the deck-head … Personally I [was] profoundly grateful to those of my officers who battled so well with this task of monstrous proportions.

A Walrus amphibian plane, pictured in June 1945. The clunky-looking Walrus had an anaemic top speed but proved invaluable in rescuing downed Allied airmen in the water far from the carriers. (HMSO/Public Domain)

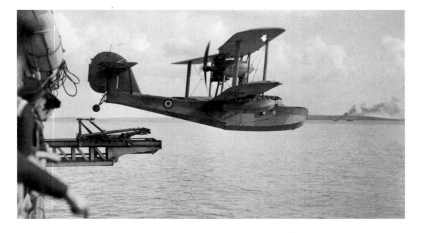

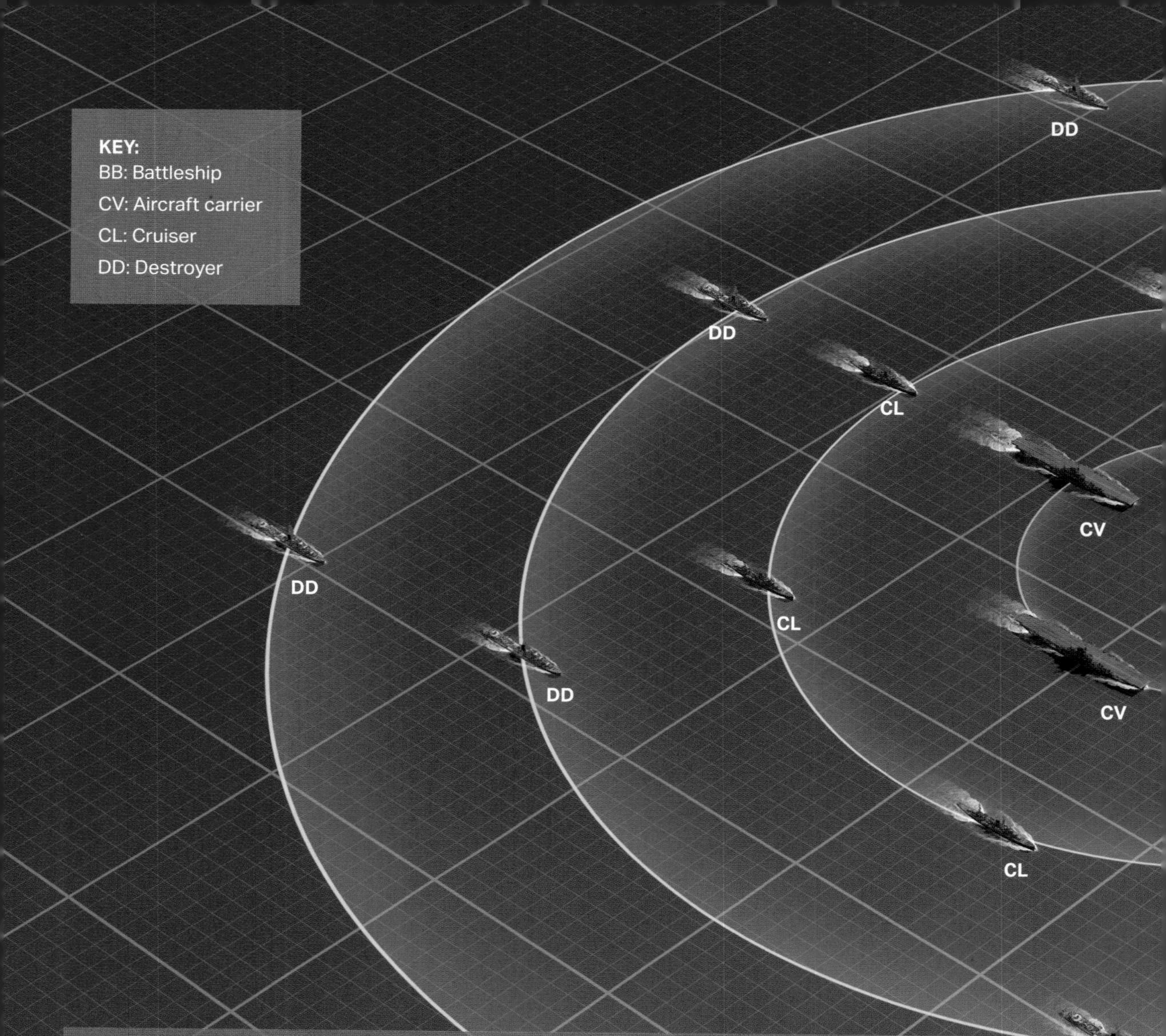

DD

DD

CL

DD

CV

DD

CL

CV

DD

CL

DD

TASK FORCE 57 COMBAT FORMATION

By 1945 Fraser's BPF had adopted the USN's updated tactical manual *USF-10 Current Tactical Orders and Doctrine US Fleet*. The BPF used the US tactical formations within *USF-10*, but also employed their own custom circular formations adapted from the USN style, which the BPF designated 5A, 5B and 5C.

The formation's ships cruised in concentric circles. Each circle was designated based on its distance in yards from the centre of the circle. For example, to steam in circle 2 meant to steam 2,000 yards outward from the centre of a 4,000-yard-wide circle. Battleships cruised with 1,000 yards between each other, compared to 600 yards for cruisers and 400 yards for destroyers.

The battleships and cruisers mounted the longest-ranged anti-aircraft guns, the 5.25in guns. Maximum anti-aircraft range was 24,070 yards (11.9nm) and maximum anti-aircraft ceiling was 41,000ft (6.75nm). Therefore, anti-aircraft envelope over the cruising formation theoretically extended 11.9nm from every battleship and cruiser and a maximum of 6.75nm in altitude above every battleship and cruiser. Realistically, the effectiveness of the anti-aircraft fire faded with increasing distance from its source.

During *Iceberg*, Task Force 57 overwhelmingly deployed in the USN's **Cruising Disposition 5B**, or CD 5B. The carriers were deployed in a diamond formation in circle 2.5, battleships and cruisers in circle 3.5, and destroyers

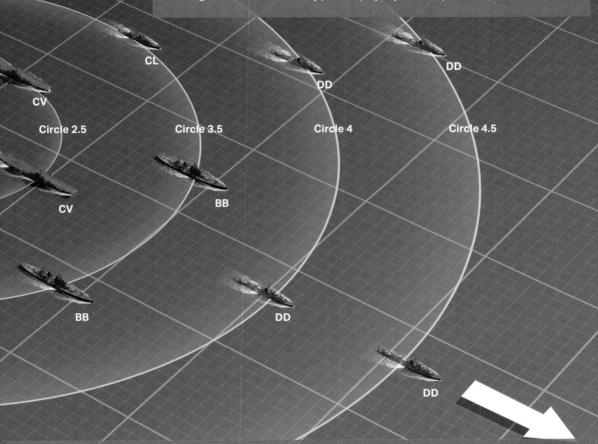

RADIO COMMUNICATIONS

The Fleet Guide, cruising in the centre of the formation, orders changes in speed and course primarily through TBS radio, which has a c.10nm range and can easily reach the destroyer screen on Circle 4.5 perimeter, as Circle 4.5 is only 2.22nm from the fleet guide, which therefore also means no ship in the entire formation is ever more than 4.44nm from any other ship in the formation. This means TBS radio transmitted from any ship in the 5B cruising formation can be readily picked up by any other ship in the formation.

on circles 4 and 4.5. The carriers' formation was designed to give as much room as possible for the carriers to conduct air operations, while still being relatively defensible by their escorts.

Task Force 57 had numerous other cruising formations to draw from. Three related formations are described below:

Cruising Disposition 5A was intended to defend against aircraft and submarines. In 5A, the four carriers cruised in circle 2, with a cruiser at the centre as the task force guide. The battleships and remaining cruisers would deploy on circle 5, with the destroyers on circle 8.

Cruising Disposition 5C was intended for night steaming and was primarily concerned with defending against submarines. A cruiser would steam in the centre, with the four carriers in circle 2. Destroyers, battleships and remaining cruisers would deploy on circle 6.

Cruising Disposition 5F was intended for daylight steaming when air attack was expected. The guide cruiser and carriers deployed as usual, but two battleships and two cruisers would form a 4,000-yard-wide square centred on the guide cruiser. Each carrier would be trailed tightly astern by a so-designated 'KK' destroyer to provide direct support against kamikazes. The remaining cruisers and destroyers would deploy on circle 7.

DOCTRINE

The BPF's primary formation, the fast carrier task force, was officially commanded by Vice Admiral Bernard Rawlings, although in practice the task force was under the carrier commander, Rear Admiral Philip Vian. The British carrier force deliberately copied the US Fast Carrier Task Force in tactics and doctrine as much as possible. The general pattern was to close to within 100nm of the target and launch fighter sweeps, called 'Ramrods', that were timed to hit enemy airfields at dawn, followed by bomber and fighter-bomber strikes and then offensive fighter patrols that maintained aggressive air superiority patrols over the enemy airfields throughout the day. These operations would last from dawn to dusk, at which point the carriers would recover their aircraft and partially retire overnight, before reversing course and repeating the process at dawn the next day. After two to three consecutive days of air operations, fuel and ordnance would be exhausted and the carrier force would retire several hundred miles to a designated Replenishment Area rendezvous. Here a Logistic Support Group (LSG) would refuel and reprovision the force, delivering replacement planes and aircrew as needed. Replenishment lasted one to three days, following which the carriers would return to the strike zone.

The main BPF force was defended by airborne CAPs that would be directed to intercept any potential threat detected on radar. Separate high-, medium- and low-level CAPs were usually stacked over the fleet at prescribed altitudes.

Walrus floatplanes conducted Search and Rescue (SAR) missions. Screening destroyers were also detached to search the ocean for potential survivors. The knowledge that the BPF (and any nearby American forces) would go to extreme lengths to find crashed airmen helped keep morale and aggressiveness high. SAR missions were often dangerous. During an attack against Sumatra, two *Illustrious* aircraft were seen to have been shot down near a lake. Vian recalled:

> Captain Lambe, always deeply concerned for his airmen, begged that during the next operation two of his aircraft should be set aside to search the shores of the lake, while a Walrus was kept ready to pick the crews up if they were discovered. Reluctantly, I agreed. The airmen were not seen, so the rescue attempt was not made, somewhat to my relief. I felt that we were overstepping the limits of reasonable risk to the rescuers. It remained ever a problem where to draw the line.

The BPF also exploited the American tactic of 'lifeguard submarines'. These were US submarines assigned to specific areas whose mission was to find and rescue any friendly airmen who had been shot down. The BPF returned the favour by rescuing any American airmen adrift in its own patrol area.

INTELLIGENCE, COMMUNICATION AND DECEPTION

The BPF had two fully separate lines of intelligence and communication. This was a product of having two masters: the Royal Navy (both the Admiralty in London and BPF headquarters at Sydney) and the active battle fleet of the US Pacific Fleet (either the Fifth Fleet under Spruance or the Third Fleet under Halsey). There was a major difference, however, in that the BPF was explicitly subordinate to British command, but only implicitly so to American command. In any case, prolific intelligence and communications went both ways to each superior organization.

The Pacific was so vast, and its landmasses so remote or obscure, that even in 1941 many of its islands and littorals were still not charted in accurate detail. However, by 1945 the USN had amassed an enormous amount of intelligence on Pacific geography and Japanese forces. This sensitive information was exchanged freely with the BPF, including American charts and photographs. Additionally, by 1945 US cryptologists had thoroughly cracked the Imperial

Japanese Navy (IJN) Combined Fleet's codes, and the information gleaned was made privy to the BPF, although often without specifying the source.

A tactic adopted from the Americans proved particularly helpful. Before each dawn strike, each carrier air group commander would fly a preliminary Hellcat reconnaissance run over the enemy islands and choose strike targets. These would be broadcast back, and the reconnaissance commanders would remain aloft to coordinate inbound strikes, which were already aloft. Post-strike Hellcat photoreconnaissance was also standard and helped keep the intelligence situation current.

In 1918 and again in 1943 significant US battleship forces had deployed from British waters under Royal Navy control and had enthusiastically adopted British codes and signalling practices. As Home Fleet commander in 1943 Fraser had personally observed that such attitudes had gone far towards forging team unity. Now with the national situation reversed, Fraser resolved to return the favour, and for the same reasons. The Admiralty was reluctant, with First Sea Lord Admiral Sir Andrew Cunningham 'strongly of the opinion that on no account should the British Fleet use the American system of signalling'. Fraser was undeterred, appointing the like-minded Commander Richard Courage (Royal Navy) as BPF Fleet Signal Communications Officer and sending him to Washington, Pearl Harbor and Sydney to implement the new signalling system. The British were helped by the Royal Australian Navy (RAN), which had long been operating under USN procedures. Additionally, the Americans would provide each BPF ship with its own USN signals liaison team.

Deception largely involved a black-out of transmitted long-range radio under operating conditions demanding stealth. Additionally, it was well-known that Allied personnel taken captive by the Japanese were typically tortured and threatened with execution to force them to reveal information. Such knowledge, Vian reported, 'not only made casualties particularly hard to bear, but led to our aircrews being kept ignorant of details of all operations other than the particular sortie on which they were engaged. This could not but affect morale to some extent.'

LOGISTICS AND FACILITIES

Captain Harry Hopkins was named the BPF's liaison officer with the US Pacific Fleet. Hopkins immediately observed, 'Logistics is the most important aspect of the war at sea, in the Pacific', and he repeatedly stressed this when he visited the Admiralty in mid-1944.

The logistics demands placed on the BPF were no doubt its greatest challenge. In no other field did the wartime demands placed on the BPF so thoroughly outstrip what had been planned and expected. The mostly successful way the BPF handled this challenge, largely by improvisation, was arguably its most impressive feat.

The BPF's main base was at Sydney, which had two major dockyards at Garden Island and Cockatoo Island. At 1,139ft (347m) long by 147ft (45m) wide,

British Pacific Fleet flagship, battleship *Duke of York*, is seen flanked by destroyers *Wager* and *Whelp* in August 1945. *Duke of York* was carrying BPF commander-in-chief Admiral Fraser to Tokyo Bay for the surrender ceremony. (IWM A 30381)

Sydney's brand-new Captain Cook Drydock at the Garden Island Dockyard could dock any British warship. Construction had begun in May 1940. It would dock its first ship, carrier *Illustrious*, on 11 February 1945. A second Sydney drydock, the Sutherland Drydock, was 680ft long and could accept cruisers.

By 1945 Australian manpower was tapped out, an issue compounded by Australia's recalcitrant labour unions. Some 9,700 men were planned to operate BPF repair facilities in Australia. Originally half were to be British, but political hang-ups ultimately slashed this to mere hundreds with the Australians providing even less.

British planners had simply not expected the Americans' extraordinarily rapid advances, which meant Sydney was well-provisioned but also frustratingly far behind the BPF's operating zone. An American-style forward operating base would be established closer to the front lines at the Admiralty Islands' Manus atoll ('Scapa Flow with bloody palm trees'). However, the war ended before Manus was fully exploited and the US base at Leyte Gulf (Leyte-Samar or San Pedro Bay) was arguably more important to the BPF's operations.

In contrast to the marathon transoceanic voyages possible by the sailing-era Royal Navy, fuel requirements had essentially tied the steam-powered Royal Navy to established bases. Yet the Royal Navy's global network of bases, supported by the British Empire, had been fully adequate until 1941, when the system was shattered by the Japanese offensive.

In contrast, since the early 1900s the USN had studied and prepared for a Pacific-wide naval offensive under the assumption that virtually no true bases would be available for the American advance. Forty years of USN warship design and operational doctrine had therefore stressed extreme long range to almost pathological levels. US warships were designed with huge fuel tanks and highly fuel-efficient powerplants. Although at-sea replenishment had been a gimmick in other navies, the pre-war USN had expected to rely upon it. By mid-war the Americans had thoroughly drilled themselves in the art of abeam refuelling, which was far more efficient than the usual astern method.

By 1944 the Americans' Pacific logistic system had reached extraordinary levels. As US forces had advanced, highly trained combat engineers would

BRITISH PACIFIC FLEET LOGISTICS

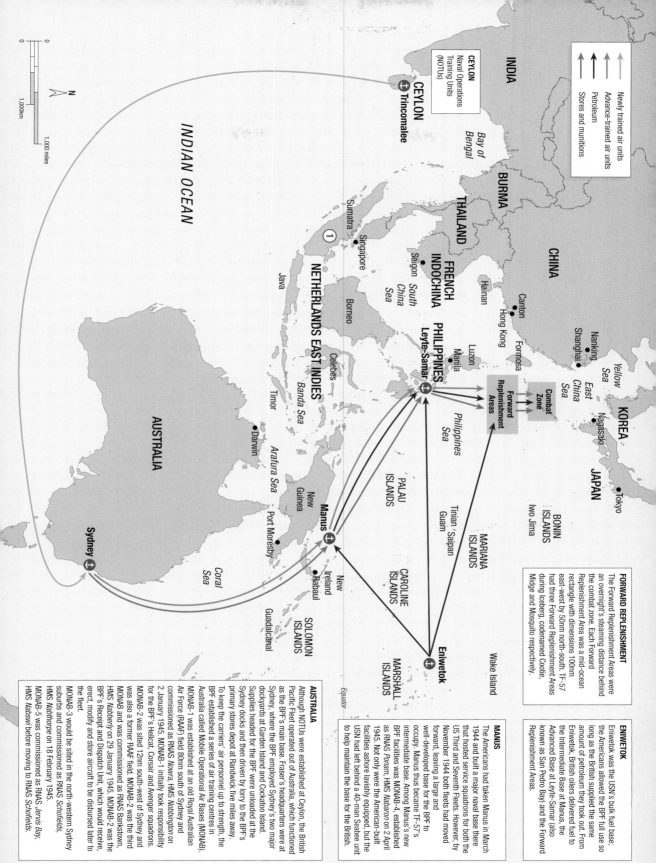

Legend

Newly trained air units
Advance-trained air units
Petroleum
Stores and munitions

CEYLON
Naval Operations
Training Units
(NOTUs)

N
0 — 1,000km
0 — 1,000 miles

INDIA

CEYLON
✚ Trincomalee

Bay of
Bengal

BURMA

THAILAND

CHINA

Yellow
Sea

KOREA

• Tokyo

JAPAN

Nanking •
Shanghai •

East
China
Sea

• Nagasaki

INDIAN OCEAN

Sumatra

Singapore

①

FRENCH
INDOCHINA

Saigon •

South
China
Sea

Hainan

Canton •

Hong Kong •

Formosa

Luzon

Manila •

PHILIPPINES
Leyte-Samar
✚

Bonn
ISLANDS

Iwo Jima

NETHERLANDS EAST INDIES

Java

Borneo

Celebes

Banda Sea

Timor

Arafura
Sea

Darwin •

Philippines
Sea

PALAU
ISLANDS

Forward
Replenishment
Areas

Combat
Zone

Tinian / Saipan
Guam

MARIANA
ISLANDS

Wake Island

AUSTRALIA

New
Guinea

Port Moresby •

Manus
✚

New
Ireland

Rabaul •

Coral
Sea

Guadalcanal

SOLOMON
ISLANDS

CAROLINE
ISLANDS

Eniwetok
✚

MARSHALL
ISLANDS

Sydney
✚

Equator

FORWARD REPLENISHMENT
The Forward Replenishment Areas were an overnight's steaming distance behind the combat zone. Each Forward Replenishment Area was a mid-ocean rectangle with dimensions 100nm east-west by 50nm north-south. TF-57 had three Forward Replenishment Areas during Iceberg, codenamed Cootie, Midge and Mosquito respectively.

ENIWETOK
Eniwetok was the USN's bulk fuel base; the Americans allowed the BPF full use so long as the British supplied the same amount of petroleum they took out. From Eniwetok, British oilers delivered fuel to the Intermediate Base at Manus, the Advanced Base at Leyte-Samar (also known as San Pedro Bay) and the Forward Replenishment Areas.

MANUS
The Americans had taken Manus in March 1944 and built a major naval base there that hosted service squadrons for both the US Third and Seventh Fleets. However, by November 1944 both fleets had moved forward, leaving a large and well-developed base for the BPF to occupy. Manus thus became TF-57's intermediate base. Among Manus's new BPF facilities was MONAB-4, established as RNAS *Nabaron* on 2 April 1945. Not only were the American-built facilities ashore lavishly equipped, but the USN had left behind a 40-man Seabee unit to help maintain the base for the British.

AUSTRALIA
Although NOTUs were established at Ceylon, the British Pacific Fleet operated out of Australia, which functioned as the BPF's main base. Fraser's headquarters were at Sydney, where the BPF employed Sydney's two major dockyards at Garden Island and Cockatoo Island. Supplies headed for the BPF were unloaded at the Sydney docks and then driven by lorry to the BPF's primary stores depot at Randwick five miles away.
To keep the carriers' air personnel up to strength, the BPF established a series of air training centres in Australia called Mobile Operational Air Bases (MONAB). MONAB-1 was established at an old Royal Australian Air Force (RAAF) field 80nm south of Sydney and commissioned as RNAS *Nowra*. HMS *Nabbington* on 2 January 1945. MONAB-1 initially took responsibility for the BPF's Hellcat, Corsair and Avenger squadrons. MONAB-2 was sited 12nm south-west of Sydney and was also a former RAAF field. MONAB-2 was the third MONAB and was commissioned as RNAS Bankstown, HMS *Nabberly* on 29 January 1945. MONAB-2 was the BPF's Receipt and Dispatch Unit, which would receive, erect, modify and store aircraft to be disbursed later to the fleet.
MONAB-3 would be sited in the north-western Sydney suburbs and commissioned as RNAS *Schofields*, HMS *Nabthorpe* on 1 March 1945. MONAB-5 was commissioned as RNAS *Jervis Bay*, HMS *Nabswi* before moving to RNAS *Schofields*.

carve impressive intermediate and advance bases out of desolate Pacific islands, often while still under fire. These new bases were then supplied by regularly scheduled civilian convoys from the US West Coast. Faster, better-armed and better-escorted USN service squadrons then forwarded the fuel and provisions to US warships in the combat zones, usually replenishing underway as a matter of procedure. This allowed US combat fleets to remain at sea for weeks or even months at a time, a phenomenon not seen since the sailing era. Floating repair facilities at the advanced bases allowed all but the worst damage to be repaired near the front. This incredible new paradigm allowed a swift, relentless and unpredictable operational tempo that completely overwhelmed Japanese defensive strategy and even caught the Americans by surprise.

To British observers, it was apparent the Americans were forging a revolutionary new system of warfare that must be emulated, if only to keep from falling farther behind. Unfortunately, available British shipping remained scarce, even though Britain's imports had been reduced from a pre-war 60 million tons/year to a wartime low of merely 24 million tons. According to Royal Navy historian S. W. Roskill, 'Planning to get the [British] fleet's supplies afloat had, in fact, been in progress since 1936, and it was only the harsh realities of the war, and the very heavy losses our Merchant Navy had suffered, which had prevented more being done to implement these plans.'

Although the late-war USN logistic system seemed lavishly provisioned to outsiders, there remained precious little slack that could be gifted to new commitments. Therefore, under the terms stipulated at the Quadrant Conference, the USN would allow free use of its bulk fuel supply (provided the Royal Navy contributed as much as it consumed) but insisted the BPF maintain its own service squadron and be self-sufficient in all other forms of provision. However, by January 1945 Nimitz's staff agreed that 'a broader interpretation of the [self-sufficiency] directive would [be] most desirable both for efficiency and for preservation of friendly relations'. Nimitz instructed his liaison officer to inform Fraser 'we would

Task Force 37 refuels at sea, as viewed from cruiser *Black Prince* in August 1945. Royal Navy officers marvelled at the Japanese submarine force's refusal to try to interfere in the slow and dangerous replenishment operations, a situation the Germans would hardly have passed up. (IWM 30386)

make it work regardless of anything' and as the BPF ramped up combat operations the Americans donated considerable amounts of logistic services 'under the table'.

The BPF's dedicated service squadron, called the Fleet Train, was designated TF-112 and would be commanded by Rear Admiral D. B. Fisher. According to *Victorious*'s Captain Michael Denny:

> Afloat support was something which, in the Royal Navy, had been totally neglected before the war. Admiral Fisher made a terrific job of it, frankly, we all expected it to be an awful mess ... It was as near perfect as possible with what he had to use. It had never been worked out before – but he did it.

By March 1945 the BPF's Fleet Train totalled 65 ships, including tankers, armament stores issuing ships (ASIS), victualling stores issuing ships (VSIS), naval stores issuing ships (NSIS), hospital ships, water distilling ships, colliers, tugs and escorting ships. Repair and maintenance ships were run by the Royal Navy, while some tankers and stores ships belonged to the Royal Fleet Auxiliary, essentially a civilian shipping line the Admiralty owned and operated.

The part of the Fleet Train that replenished the carrier force while underway was called the Logistic Support Group (LSG). As late as early 1945, the Royal Navy was still refuelling at sea via the astern method, in which floating hoses were trailed behind the tanker to the ship to be refuelled. 'It was an awkward and unseaman-like business,' Vian rued. 'For some reason we had failed to benefit from American experience to fit our tankers and warships with the necessary tackle to employ [the American] method. We were to suffer for it until we did so.' Unlike the purpose-built US oilers, British tankers required jury-rigging to transfer petroleum underway, and often 'the fuelling gear would become entangled, or hoses would burst'. Such foul-ups could add up to six hours to the already slow fuelling times, and the British carriers would often have to race through the night to reach their assigned launch points in time, further exacerbating the fuel situation.

However, by early July 1945 the BPF was confidently relying on American-style abeam refuelling. Even *King George V* and the cruisers could refuel their screening destroyers at 150 tons and 100 tons per hour respectively. After 15 July *King George V* would always refuel from tankers via the abeam method, averaging 400 tons per hour. According to Roskill: 'The Americans ... taught us that modern warships, suitably supported, could keep the seas and engage continuously in active operations for upwards of two months – a feat which, in 1939, we never would have considered practicable.'

Aircraft Maintenance Carriers

In 1939 the Royal Navy ordered a new light carrier to serve as an aircraft repair ship. Entering service in June 1943, HMS *Unicorn* displaced 16,500 tons and had a top speed of 24 knots. *Unicorn* deployed to the Eastern Fleet in January 1944 and joined the BPF in February 1945.

LOGISTIC SUPPORT GROUP REPLENISHMENT FORMATION

Each LSG comprised three to four tankers, escorted by half a dozen frigates, sloops and corvettes. The LSG's tankers steamed in line across at 10 knots, with 2,000 yards in between each other. The LSG's escort vessels would steam in circle 8, which is 8,000 yards from the centre of the formation. This gave the LSG a circular formation 7.9nm in diameter.

Two to three ships at a time would approach a tanker to replenish. A British tanker could generally refuel a destroyer on each beam and a single heavy ship astern simultaneously.

After *Unicorn*, the incomplete Colossus-class light carrier *Pioneer* was converted into an aircraft maintenance carrier. Unlike *Unicorn*, *Pioneer* lacked air control facilities, catapults and arrestor gear. Unable to conduct flight operations, the carrier had to crane aircraft aboard. *Pioneer* arrived in the Pacific in May 1945. *Unicorn* and *Pioneer* largely operated out of Manus and Leyte-Samar.

Escort Carriers

Nine escort carriers served with the Fleet Train as 30th Aircraft Carrier Squadron (30 ACS), commanded by Commodore William P. Carne. Of these, the four Attacker-class and four Ruler-class carriers were American-built and acquired under Lend-Lease. A single carrier, the Nairana-class HMS *Vindex*, had been built in Britain. All nine escort carriers displaced around 11,000 tons, and carried about 20 aircraft at 17–18 knots. The escort carriers were used both to ferry planes to the main carrier force, and to provide air cover for the Fleet Train itself. During replenishment operations, a replenishment group escort carrier would also take over all daily air patrols, allowing the fleet carriers' air groups to get some rest.

Convoy Escorts

Protecting the Fleet Train were 20-knot sloops and frigates and 15-knot corvettes. These were designed for anti-air and anti-submarine convoy defence, and intentionally sacrificed speed for range. The major types assigned to the BPF were the 1,025-ton Bathurst-class corvettes, which escorted long-haul convoys, and the 1,350-ton Black Swan-class sloops and 1,370-ton River-class frigates, which directly escorted the LSGs to and from the Replenishment Areas.

Escort carriers HMS *Slinger* and HMS *Speaker* en route to the Pacific in early 1945. The escort carriers were too slow and vulnerable to conduct front-line combat with the fleet carriers but were invaluable for supply and defence during replenishment operations. (IWM A 28887)

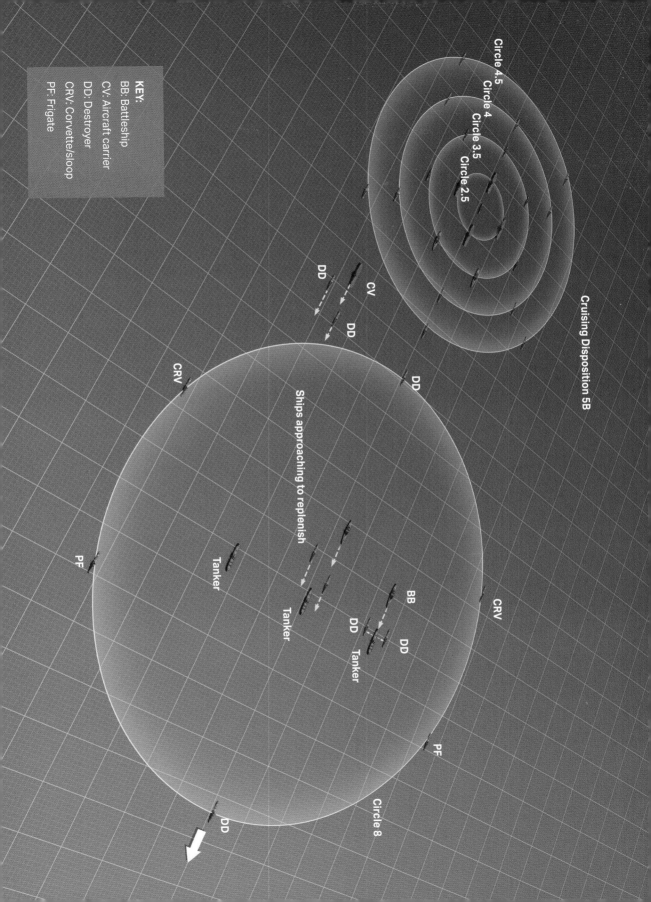

KEY:
BB: Battleship
CV: Aircraft carrier
DD: Destroyer
CRV: Corvette/sloop
PF: Frigate

Cruising Disposition 5B

Circle 4.5
Circle 4
Circle 3.5
Circle 2.5

DD
CV
DD
DD

CRV

Ships approaching to replenish

Tanker
Tanker

BB
DD
Tanker
DD

CRV

PF

PF

Circle 8

DD

THE FLEET IN COMBAT

Lieutenant C. J. Lavender, Royal Naval Volunteer Reserve (RNVR), poses in front of his Hellcat fighter during the Sumatra strikes, 18 January 1945. The Hellcat easily outclassed most Japanese aircraft it would face. (Photo by Reuben Saidman/Popperfoto via Getty Images)

The British Pacific Fleet was officially established on 22 November 1944. Its primary formation, the fast carrier striking force, would engage in training raids during late 1944 and early 1945, before finally being committed to its first major campaign, the invasion of Okinawa. Codenamed Operation *Iceberg*, the BPF's carrier striking force would engage in two tours off Okinawa between March and May 1945. Then between July and August 1945 the carrier striking force would fight alongside Halsey's Third Fleet, launching air and surface bombardments of the Japanese Home Islands. In the meantime, BPF submarine forces would operate farther south, scoring notable victories against Japan's surviving heavy cruisers. Finally, the BPF would engage in the surrender and liberation operations in August and September 1945.

Perhaps most of all the BPF is remembered for facing the kamikaze threat. From March through August 1945, Japanese air and naval forces would sacrifice over 2,000 kamikazes off Okinawa and the Home Islands in one of the most violent aerial counteroffensives ever mounted.

Once a kamikaze entered its final dive, only evasive manoeuvres or the kamikaze's annihilation could prevent a hit. Standard anti-aircraft tactics of deflecting an attacker or interfering with the aim of its projectile did not work when the aircraft itself was the ordnance to be expended. One drawback to using kamikazes was that they were much flimsier and lower-velocity than bombs or torpedoes, meaning the planes themselves generally did not penetrate armour, making kamikazes incapable of sinking an armoured warship. However, when they exploded topside they threw large amounts of metal shrapnel and flaming gasoline, which caused particularly horrific injuries and badly damaged morale.

Beginning on 4 January 1945, Admiral Fraser visited battleship *New Mexico* as a distinguished observer to the US Seventh Fleet's Lingayen Gulf landings. Just two days later, Fraser was observing from *New Mexico*'s bridge when a kamikaze slammed into it, causing massive carnage. Just moments earlier Fraser had been standing at the portside impact location before walking to the starboard side to observe the US landings. The kamikaze strike killed 30 men, including *New Mexico*'s captain and Churchill's personal envoy, General Sir Herbert Lumsden. A shaken Fraser was left unhurt, but his assistant secretary was killed. Fraser considered these losses 'a high price to pay for personal experience' but his near-death encounter with a kamikaze imparted instant credibility to those he would shortly order into harm's way.

The Sumatran Raids, 17 December 1944– 29 January 1945

The BPF had been scheduled to depart for its new Australian headquarters in December 1944, but it would have arrived still unable to conduct combat operations. Therefore, while Fraser was visiting Nimitz in Hawaii, he ordered the BPF, still based in the Indian Ocean, to conduct practice strikes against the Japanese-controlled oil refineries on the island of Sumatra, Netherlands East Indies. The strikes against these targets would serve several functions. First and most importantly, they would allow the BPF and particularly its largely untrained aircrew to gain seasoning in live combat. Secondly, the oil refineries themselves were much more vulnerable to the precision bombing of carrier aircraft than they were to high-altitude heavy bombers. Finally, they were genuinely valuable targets, whose damage would hurt the Japanese war economy a great deal.

The BPF commenced its first official combat mission, Operation *Robson*, on 17 December 1944. Sortieing from Ceylon were carriers *Indomitable* and *Illustrious*, three cruisers and six destroyers. This embryonic carrier strike force was designated Task Force 67. Aboard the carriers were 103 aircraft. Vice Admiral Rawlings was severely ill at the time and unable to go to sea, thus tactical command for the Sumatran raids devolved onto the carrier squadron commander, Rear Admiral Phillip Vian, who flew his flag aboard *Indomitable*.

On 20 December TF-67 reached the entrance to the Straits of Malacca, the designated launch point. Despite rainy, overcast weather, by 0715hrs TF-67 had launched 27 Avengers, each armed with four 500lb bombs, along with an escort of 28 Corsair and Hellcat fighters. Although only half of Vian's force had been launched, the 55-plane strike was already the largest single carrier strike the Royal Navy had yet conducted. However, thick rain and nearly sea-level clouds covered the primary target, so the strike was diverted to port facilities at Belawan Deli. The attack was a complete surprise, resulting in modest anti-aircraft fire and no enemy fighters. After the first strike was returned, a fighter sweep struck airfields on Sabang island, as well as the port of Kota Raja on Sumatra. TF-67 then returned to Ceylon.

After TF-67 returned to Ceylon on 22 December the BPF prepared a follow-up strike. For Operation *Lentil*, Vian would command three carriers. Aboard carriers *Indomitable*, *Victorious* and *Indefatigable* were 178 aircraft, with the carriers now escorted by four cruisers and eight destroyers. This second formation was designated TF-65 and departed from Ceylon on 1 January 1945. This time TF-65 would be gifted with clear weather for the attack.

Vian's carriers launched on 4 January. As per doctrine, a Ramrod fighter sweep pre-emptively struck the airfields surrounding the main target. The main strike of Avengers, escorted by its own fighters, then attacked the refinery. This strike was much more successful, with the refinery 'left burning furiously' and 16 enemy fighters either shot down in the air or destroyed on the ground at their airfields. A single plane was lost, but its crew was recovered.

Vian was increasingly pleased with the performance of his carrier force. On 16 January 1945 the BPF sortied one last time from Ceylon. Vian's carriers would strike Palembang while en route to Sydney. By now Vian's fleet comprised carriers *Indomitable*, *Victorious*, *Indefatigable* and *Illustrious*, battleship *King George V*, cruisers *Argonaut*, *Black Prince* and *Euryalus*, and ten destroyers. TF-67 conducted an at-sea refuelling on 20 January, then headed for the target.

Victorious aircraft strike the Japanese-occupied oil refineries at Palembang, Sumatra, in January 1945. Although the refinery raids provided valuable practice for the newly established BPF, they also had a strategic effect by cutting into Japanese oil production. (IWM A 29244)

However, a major tropical front closed in and Vian was forced to postpone air operations several days. The weather finally cleared late on 23 January. By dawn the next morning the weather was 'crystal clear', and the Sumatran mountains were visible to the east.

At 0615hrs, on 24 January, TF-67 carriers began launching. The main target for this mission, dubbed Operation *Meridian I*, was the refinery at Pladjoe. It was allotted a well-escorted strike force of 43 Avengers, each armed with the standard four 500lb bombs. Preceding the main strike was the usual Ramrod fighter sweep against enemy airfields, while four Avengers also bombed the main airbase at Mana. By 0700hrs the main strike was away. TF-67 was 35nm from the Sumatran coast. Its aircraft would then have to climb above the 11,000ft Sumatran mountains and proceed another 100nm inland.

Just short of the target, barrage balloons were sighted over the refinery and anti-aircraft guns opened fire. Japanese fighters appeared overhead and dived on the Avenger strike but were met by the Avengers' escort. Some of the Avengers dived through the barrage balloon cables, while others released their bombs above the balloons. In any case, enough damage was done to cut the refinery's output in half. The Ramrod sweep had destroyed 34 enemy fighters on the ground, but enough escaped to ambush the retiring but escorted Avenger strike. The British claimed 14 total Japanese planes shot down before the strike escaped safely back to the waiting carriers. However, British losses were six Corsairs, two Avengers and one Hellcat.

On 24–25 January the strike force made one last at-sea refuelling, allowing Vian to make one final attack on Palembang before heading for Sydney. Aerial tactics were adjusted, with two separate fighter sweeps timed to arrive simultaneously over the two main Japanese airbases. The bombers' route was also re-arranged to avoid areas discovered to be heavy with anti-aircraft batteries. Finally, it was assumed that the Japanese would attack the British carriers now known to be in the area, and so the standing CAP was greatly strengthened.

Operation *Meridian II* opened at dawn on 29 January. By 0730hrs the British carriers had launched over 100 planes against the enemy. The main target was the Soengei Gerong refinery. The Ramrod fighter sweeps arrived on time at 0830hrs, but the Japanese were already airborne and waiting, and large air battles broke out. Fireflies raced ahead of the Avenger strike and shot down several barrage balloons. The Avengers caused severe damage to the refinery, interrupting all production until late March. However, two Avengers were destroyed by balloon cables, including the wing leader. Two Avengers shot down Japanese aircraft in dogfights.

Japanese twin-engine bombers counterattacked. After running battles with the CAP, several managed to get close enough to commence low-altitude attack runs against *Illustrious* and *Indomitable*. These were shot down before they could score a hit. However, friendly anti-aircraft fire struck *Illustrious*, killing 12 men and wounding 21. The British claimed 30 Japanese planes shot down to all causes, plus another 38 destroyed at their airfields.

With good weather now forecast and the defending Japanese air strength battered, the damaged enemy refinery now appeared on the verge of complete destruction. 'The stage was all set for a final raid,' Vian claimed. However, the fleet was too low on fuel to linger any longer and would have to put into Fremantle before continuing to Sydney. The BPF had achieved local superiority, yet a dire fuel situation would force it to retire just as total supremacy appeared within reach. The frustrating situation would repeat itself throughout the rest of the war.

A total of 41 BPF aircraft were lost during the two *Meridian* raids, with 16 planes lost in combat and 25 to operational causes. A total of 30 aircrew were killed or missing. After the war it was learned that at least nine British airmen had been taken captive and later executed.

Vian's force arrived at Sydney on 10 February 1945. Fortunately, the maintenance aircraft carrier *Unicorn* had just made harbour days earlier and was able to repair and replace the fleet carriers' air groups.

At Sydney, Vian relinquished Task Force command to a recovered Vice Admiral Rawlings, who broke his flag aboard *King George V*. Vian remained as carrier squadron commander. Until now the BPF had been using traditional British signals and procedures, but from now on they would have to retrain with the American signals that Fraser had embraced. 'The American battle squadron which had joined the Grand Fleet in the First World War had adopted our signal system,' Vian admitted. 'Now it was our turn. None of us pretended to like it.'

Operation *Iceberg I*, 25 March–20 April 1945

On 28 February 1945 the BPF carrier strike force, now designated TF-113, departed Sydney for Manus. TF-113 arrived at its new forward base on 7 March 1945, then conducted exercises while patiently waiting for the Americans' official word to join *Iceberg*.

Pom-pom practice aboard battleship HMS *Howe* off New Zealand, January 1945. Unfortunately the 2-pdr pom-poms and the 20mm Oerlikons were too weak to disintegrate kamikazes in mid-air, which required at least the Bofors 40mm cannon. (IWM A 28851)

Although the Americans had already converted Manus into a significant base out of virtually nothing, Vian found Manus a disappointment. Only 27 of the 69 ships allocated to the Fleet Train had arrived, partly because of the persistent longshoreman strikes at Sydney. Among the missing vessels was the water ship, forcing the BPF warships to rely on their own insufficient condensers. A long, unpleasant swell ran through most of the anchorage, making provisioning a difficult process. As for Rawlings, he found Manus's climate so disagreeable that his report to the Admiralty wondered 'under what circumstance and whose whimsical conception these islands should have been named in honour of Their Lordships'.

Only on 14 March did King finally send the message officially authorizing the BPF to participate in Operation *Iceberg* under Spruance's US Fifth Fleet. Apparently even then King had still not abandoned his idea that the BPF should be deployed in a more subsidiary theatre, because his authorizing message also required that the BPF make sure that it could fully disengage and be re-deployed elsewhere on seven days' notice.

Nevertheless, Rawlings promptly messaged Nimitz: 'I hereby report TF-113 and TF-112 for duty in accordance with orders received from C-in-C British Pacific Fleet … It is with a feeling of great pride and pleasure that the British Pacific Fleet joins the US Naval Forces under your command.' To this Nimitz responded, 'The

United States Fleet welcomes the British Carrier Task Force and attached units which will greatly add to our power to strike the enemy and will also show our unity of purpose in the war against Japan.'

On 17 March, an advanced detachment of the Fleet Train, totalling 15 ships and escorted by three escort carriers and several frigates, departed Manus en route for Ulithi. Rawlings' carrier force, now re-designated Task Force 57, departed Manus the following day, 18 March. The replenishment of Rawlings' force during *Iceberg* would be assigned to the Logistic Support Group (TG-112.2) of five escort carriers, five oilers and four chartered merchantmen, escorted by four destroyers, four sloops and three frigates.

Now fully fuelled, TF-57 sortied from Ulithi on 23 March and proceeded towards its assigned combat area. TF-57 comprised four fast carriers, fast battleships *Howe* and *King George V*, five cruisers and 11 destroyers. This closely equalled a single US fast carrier Task Group in size, although TF-57 carried only 244 carrier planes compared to around 320 for a US Task Group.

The planned US invasion of Okinawa was dubbed Operation *Iceberg*. Okinawa's central location in relation to surrounding Japanese air power made it an extremely difficult naval objective. Over 3,000 Japanese aircraft were massed at Kyushu's 55 airfields 350nm to the north-east. Another 400 Japanese planes were based at Formosa's 65 airfields 350nm to the west-south-west. Halfway between Okinawa and Formosa was the Sakashima Gunto archipelago, which boasted another six Japanese airfields 230nm from Okinawa.

On 1 April 1945 (L-Day) Spruance's US Fifth Fleet would assault Okinawa's Hagushi beaches with four divisions of the US Tenth Army. The naval force itself would remain off Okinawa providing air, gunfire and logistic support until Okinawa was secured. Fifth Fleet was composed of many different combat and support Task Forces organized by mission. Most of Fifth Fleet consisted of TF-51, the overall amphibious force and amphibious support force (over 1,000 vessels under Vice Admiral Richmond K. Turner). TF-51 would surround Okinawa, although TF-51's main assault shipping forces TF-53 and TF-55 mostly occupied a large anchorage just off the landing zones at south-western Okinawa's Hagushi beaches.

Spruance's primary battle fleet was Vice Admiral Marc Mitscher's US Fast Carrier Task Force. Designated TF-58, it comprised 17 fast carriers, eight fast battleships, 15 cruisers and 81 destroyers in four Task Groups that embarked 1,170 front-line carrier aircraft. TF-58 would cruise an area 75–150nm east-north-east of Okinawa, where it was astride the Kyushu-Okinawa air route and could wage major offensive and defensive air missions in direct support of the entire Fleet and Tenth Army ashore.

In an inspired move, Spruance assigned his BPF contingent, Rawlings' TF-57, to suppress Japanese air power in the Sakashima Gunto archipelago, effectively covering the invasion fleet's extended left flank. TF-57 would operate 250–300nm south-west of Okinawa, generally launching its strikes from a position

British Pacific Fleet destroyers *Queensborough*, *Quality* and *Quadrant* off Auckland, New Zealand, in January 1945. The Q-class destroyers mostly escorted the carrier strike force during its major operations against the Sakashima Gunto and mainland Japan. (Photo 12/Universal Images Group via Getty Images)

100nm south-east of the Sakashima chain. The smaller, less-experienced TF-57 therefore received a secondary but still important strategic mission that directly supported Fifth Fleet's main operations, but without being irreplaceably vital to the larger fleet's ultimate success. It also placed TF-57 on the farther, weaker side of the impending air-sea campaign and well outside the staggering concentration of Japanese air power massing on Kyushu. Finally, TF-57's physical separation from Spruance's US task forces (about 200nm) was great enough to satisfy prevailing British political sentiments demanding nominal independence, while still remaining within mutual support range.

Back on 20 January 1945, the Japanese high command (IGHQ) had published its latest 'Outline of Army and Navy Operations'. A new perimeter defence zone was established, to include Iwo Jima, Formosa, Okinawa, southern Korea and the Shanghai region. The primary defensive effort would be in the Ryukyus. IGHQ's defensive plans were to be complete by March 1945, the date they expected an invasion of Okinawa, the Ryukyus' largest and most important island. Okinawa would be defended on land by Lieutenant-General Mitsuru Ushijima's Imperial Japanese Army's (IJA) 32nd Army, comprising a total of 77,000 regular troops and another 20,000 conscripted Okinawans.

Japanese air power would be hoarded until the Okinawa landings were underway. The enemy invasion fleet would then be attacked and destroyed 'primarily by sea and air special attack units' (that is, suicide attacks). Japanese air power at Kyushu encompassed three large IJN air fleets (the Fifth, Third, and Tenth) and the IJAAF Sixth Air Army. These would largely be thrown at the US invasion fleet and US fast carriers directly off Okinawa, but many would also attack TF-57 off the Sakashimas.

Based in Formosa were the IJN First Air Fleet and IJAAF 8th Air Division. Many of these units would be shuttled through the Sakashimas to attack US Fifth Fleet and TF-57. The Sakashimas' six airfields were located on two islands. Ishigaki Island hosted Ishigaki Main, Miyara and Hegina airfields, of which Ishigaki Main was paved and the others grass. Defending Ishigaki Main were

26 heavy and 66 light anti-aircraft guns. Miyako Island boasted three paved airbases at Hirara, Nobara and Sukuma. Hirara, the largest, had 12 heavy and 54 light anti-aircraft guns, with additional light batteries defending Nobara and Sukuma.

To keep Sakashima air power suppressed, TF-57 would fly daily missions over the airfields, bombing airstrips and strafing parked aircraft, while any planes that got aloft in daylight would be aggressively engaged by standing offensive fighter patrols cruising overhead.

Iceberg essentially began on 25 March, when US Fifth Fleet began its massive pre-landing bombardments of Okinawa. That same day TF-57 undertook one last at-sea replenishment. By 0615hrs on 26 March, TF-57 had reached its flying-off point 100nm south of the Sakashimas and duly launched a 48-plane 'Ramrod' fighter sweep against the airfields at Ishigaki and Miyako islands. The sweep was followed by two strikes totalling 33 Corsairs and Avengers, plus escorting Hellcats. However, throughout 26 March, TF-57 was dogged by patrolling USN PB4Y-1 bombers that drifted into TF-57 airspace without activating their IFF (Identification Friend or Foe) equipment. That evening TF-57 withdrew south-east for the night, having lost nine planes and three airmen.

In the early dark of 27 March, a Japanese moonlight snooper was detected by radar. Although lacking formal night training, an experienced pilot was dispatched in a Hellcat to intercept it. The Hellcat made visual detection before losing the snooper in the clouds. The incident apparently convinced the Japanese that the BPF had night fighter capabilities, as Japanese aircraft never engaged TF-57 at night again.

At dawn TF-57 launched a Ramrod fighter sweep of 24 Hellcats and Corsairs. The fighters were again followed by two strikes of 24 Avengers and four Fireflies each against runways and airbase buildings, plus previously undamaged radio stations, barracks and airplane dispersal areas. Two TF-57 aircraft had been lost

TASK FORCE 57 COMMAND STRUCTURE DURING *ICEBERG*

Although Vice Admiral Rawlings commanded Task Force 57 at sea, he recognized that TF-57 was a carrier force and its movements should conform to the operational needs of the carriers. Rawlings therefore normally ceded daytime tactical command of TF-57 to Rear Admiral Philip Vian, who commanded 1st Aircraft Carrier Squadron (1 ACS). Each fleet carrier deployed a specific fighter wing.

As 1 ACS commander, Vian usually held tactical control of the carrier's escorts, and thus the entire formation. This included battleships *King George V* and *Howe* of the 1st Battle Squadron (directly commanded by Rawlings), Rear Admiral E. J. P. Brind's 4th Cruiser Squadron and TF-57's destroyers in the 4th, 25th and 27th Destroyer Flotillas.

Because TF-57's carriers could not conduct flight operations at night, Rawlings resumed tactical command of TF-57 during night-time hours. Rawlings also directly commanded any TF-57 surface detachments that included his flagship *King George V*.

in combat, plus another six operationally. Deployed near the Sakashimas was US lifeguard submarine *Kingfish*, which would rescue several British airmen, while destroyer *Undine*, dispatched 56nm from the carriers, would rescue both a British and an American pilot.

Rawlings had planned another day of strikes and a battleship-cruiser shelling of the Ishigaki airfields, but with a typhoon predicted to interfere with the scheduled 29 March refuelling, Rawlings decided to retire and refuel one day early. TF-57 reached Support Area Midge on 28 March and began replenishment. TF-57 experimented with a newly devised refuelling method. After the BPF method proved a failure, TF-57 returned to USN-style replenishment. Refuelling was complete on the afternoon of 30 March.

TF-57 resumed Sakishima strikes on 31 March. These comprised the standard fighter sweeps followed by two Avenger strikes, except today a daytime CAP was established over the Japanese airfields. TF-57 lost a single Avenger in combat, but its crew was picked up by *Kingfisher*. Employing American 'Tomcat' tactics, Rawlings deployed cruiser *Argonaut* and destroyer *Wager* 30nm ahead and offset from the main formation. They would visually 'de-louse' returning strikes from Japanese planes trying to sneak in to the carriers.

TF-57 retired late on 31 March to prepare for the Okinawa landings the following morning. Aboard Spruance's transports was an invasion army of 182,112 troops. When all of US Fifth Fleet's combat, invasion and forward logistic groups were combined with TF-57 and all its forward logistic groups, Spruance directly or indirectly commanded over 1,600 ships in what was arguably the largest armada in history.

At 0640hrs on 1 April 1, TF-57 launched its first fighter sweep. Within ten minutes enemy aircraft were detected inbound at 8,000ft. The fighter sweep was recalled and additional fighters scrambled. Although the CAP shot down four attackers, several got through. Pursued by CAP fighters, at 0725hrs a Zero strafed *Indomitable*, killing one and wounding six, and then machine-gunned *King George V* to no effect. Three minutes later a bomb-laden Zero, pursued

A Japanese plane at sea level braves heavy flak during an attack run against the British Pacific Fleet carrier force. As always during such low-level attacks, friendly anti-aircraft fire shot into nearby ships was a problem. (IWM A 29711)

and damaged by a Seafire, dived into *Indefatigable's* armoured flight deck at the base of the island, producing a 3in dent, a fire below decks and additional extraneous damage. Flight operations resumed 37 minutes later, but 14 men had been killed and 15 wounded. Additionally, a 551lb bomb near-missed destroyer *Ulster*, breaching the hull and disabling the destroyer. *Ulster* was shortly towed to Leyte-Samar by cruiser *Gambia* and destroyer *Quiberon*.

Rawlings then launched several strikes against the Ishigaki and Hirara airfields, with British flyers claiming 14 Japanese planes destroyed. Later that afternoon, a kamikaze dived on the hard-manoeuvring *Victorious*, grazing the edge of the flight deck before cartwheeling into the sea close aboard and exploding harmlessly. The day's Japanese attacks had cost the British 15 dead and 21 wounded.

TF-57 departed for replenishment the following morning, 2 April. Rawlings nevertheless launched a

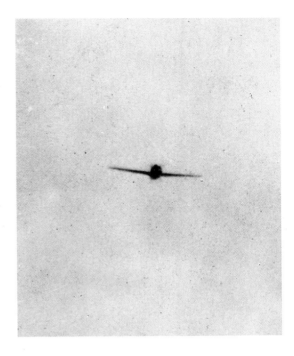

A suicidal Zero bores in on *Illustrious* during *Iceberg*. According to the original caption, only 11 seconds elapsed between the attacker emerging from the overcast to when it smashed into the water. (IWM A 29570)

17-strong dawn fighter sweep over the Sakashimas as a Parthian shot. Three Japanese planes were destroyed and one Corsair lost but its pilot recovered. As TF-57 withdrew, Nimitz signalled Rawlings congratulations for TF-57's 'illustrious' performance, to which Rawlings responded that TF-57 would pursue the enemy 'indomitably, indefatigably, and victoriously'.

Throughout *Iceberg* Rawlings would be habitually anxious to replenish quickly and efficiently, as he knew that anytime TF-57 was absent from the firing line, its assigned Sakashima suppression mission had to be assumed by the US escort carriers of TG-52.1. Not only did TG-52.1 have its own pre-existing Okinawa responsibilities, but TG-52.1's flimsy escort carriers and destroyer-escorts were much slower and more vulnerable than Rawlings' own front-line fleet units. The Royal Navy's lesser experience at underway replenishment, combined with Rawlings' deep-seated desire to live up to American expectations and his own, meant that Rawlings would often cut TF-57's replenishments short to return to the combat zone on time. As a result, TF-57 frequently returned to the Sakashima strike zone well short of full tanks. This proved the case during the 4–5 April replenishment. When unusually high seas hampered TF-57's refuelling, TF-57 was forced to return to the battle zone even though the battleships remained half empty and the carriers only had enough avgas for two days of strike operations.

TF-57 resumed Sakashima attacks early on 6 April, with strikes against Hirara, Nobara, Sukuma and Miyara airfields and coastal shipping. Late that evening a small raid of six Japanese planes attacked the carriers. Two were shot down by destroyers and three by the CAP, but a single blazing kamikaze survived to graze *Illustrious*'s bridge with its wingtip, missing Captain Lambe by nine feet. Four BPF aircraft were lost, including a Seafire and its pilot to friendly anti-aircraft fire.

On 6 April, the Japanese finally launched the first of their mass kamikaze attacks, which would be codenamed *Kikisui* ('floating chrysanthemum'). The 6–7 April *Kikisui* would ultimately hurl 699 Japanese aircraft at the Allied fleet, largely at the Americans. Of these a staggering 355 were kamikazes. Despite Allied CAPs, enough got through to cause serious damage, mostly to US radar picket destroyers. Combined Allied casualties on 6 April alone were 370 men killed and an additional 475 wounded. Although no one could know it at the time, this would be the single-day peak of Japanese kamikaze action. As *Iceberg* progressed, Japanese ability to mount such huge, coordinated single-day attacks would slowly wane. Indeed, the destruction and disorganization Allied defensive measures wrought on the Japanese air forces suspended mass kamikaze attacks for the next five days. Meanwhile, small raids would continue almost daily while the Japanese built up for their next *Kikisui* mass effort, establishing a pattern for the rest of the Okinawa battle.

TF-57 dispatched strikes to each of Ishigaki, Hirara and Nobara on 7 April, losing six planes to all causes. That same day, US carrier planes, striking from 250nm away, repulsed an approaching surface force by sinking the superbattleship *Yamato*, light cruiser *Yahagi* and four of eight destroyers. Reading the Americans' post-action reports, Rawlings observed that it 'filled the BPF with admiration, and at the same time, with envy'.

TF-57 now retired to replenish at Area Cootie over 8–9 April. By now the battle-weary *Illustrious* had gone far too long without a proper overhaul and was suffering from increasing disrepair. Limited to two overworked shafts, *Illustrious* vibrated badly. Most worryingly, much of the carrier's air group had been deployed for far too long, causing many *Illustrious* pilots to suffer from combat fatigue. Rawlings decided to detach *Illustrious* and replace the carrier with *Formidable*, which had just arrived at Leyte-Samar. Additionally, Rawlings sent ailing destroyer *Whelp* back to Leyte-Samar, and immediately found a replacement by commandeering destroyers *Undaunted* and *Whirlwind* from the replenishment group.

US intelligence now suspected that the best-trained IJN pilots were flying from Formosa to attack US Fifth Fleet off Okinawa. Spruance pleasantly surprised Rawlings by requesting TF-57 attack the Shinchuku and Matsuyama airfields in northern Formosa. Rawlings

A diving Japanese plane just misses scoring a direct hit against the hard-turning *Illustrious*, 6 April 1945. After the kamikaze's wingtip grazed *Illustrious*'s bridge, it crashed into the sea just alongside the carrier, causing its bomb to detonate. (ullstein bild via Getty Images)

agreed and planned to hit Formosa on 11 April. Considering TF-57's relatively light strength, hitting Formosa was a dangerous operation that Spruance only ordered because the situation was desperate. Spruance later told Vian that he 'had kept his fingers crossed throughout the operation'.

Rawlings had planned airstrikes for 11 April, but drizzly weather forced them to be postponed by one day. But early on 12 April TF-57 radar detected four incoming bogies. TF-57 had a CAP of 16 fighters airborne and at 0705hrs these engaged four Zeros, shooting down one. Ten minutes later TF-57 launched two strikes

of 24 Avengers and 20 fighters each against Shinchuku and an alternate target Kiirun harbour. The raids claimed six Japanese aircraft, while another eight inbound Japanese planes were engaged and annihilated by TF-57's CAP. Later two more bandits were shot down, for a 12 April score of 16 enemy planes destroyed for three British aircraft lost. TF-57 was scheduled to retire from *Iceberg I* the evening of 12 April, but with the US fleet off Okinawa getting increasingly hammered, Rawlings and Vian were reluctant to withdraw. Instead, Rawlings offered Spruance an additional, unplanned series of strikes against the Sakashima Guntos. Spruance agreed, noting 'This is fine initiative and cooperation. Cover Sakashima 16 and 17 April unless otherwise directed prior to that time.'

Early on 13 April TF-57 repelled an attack by four Japanese dive-bombers, then launched two strikes against Shinchuku and Matsuyama airfields without loss. TF-57 had capably fulfilled Nimitz's earlier prediction that British carriers would be Fifth Fleet's 'most flexible reserve'. That evening TF-57 retired for Service Area Cootie. En route TF-57 received news that US President Franklin Roosevelt had died; TF-57 would later pay its respects with memorial services aboard *Indomitable*. On 14 April, carrier *Formidable* rendezvoused with TF-57, allowing Rawlings to detach *Illustrious* for major repairs; the carrier's war was over. Replenishment was completed on 15 April and TF-57 headed back to the combat zone.

Early on 16 April TF-57 launched the first of four airstrikes against airstrips at Ishigaki, Hirara, Sukuma, Miyara, Hegina and Nobara. These were successfully cratered by 70 Avenger sorties dropping 500lb bombs and were followed by Corsair strafings. British aircraft losses were three in combat and three operationally. The following day TF-37 made three strikes against Miyako, and a Walrus picked up a downed Avenger crew barely a mile from Hirara. Four Japanese planes were destroyed trying to attack the fleet during the two-day period.

Lieutenant P. S. Cole's Corsair crash-lands aboard *Illustrious* after returning from striking Formosa. Cole survived the incident, while *Illustrious*'s crew ensured the wreckage did not start a deck fire. Task Force 57's Formosa raid was unplanned but a valuable lift to the embattled US Fifth Fleet. (IWM A 29271)

TF-57 refuelled on 18 April, before concluding its first *Iceberg* tour with one last day of unrequested Sakashima strikes on 20 April. Rawlings then retired to Leyte-Samar. Spruance later recalled:

> In spite of the fact that Admiral Rawlings and I had had no chance for a personal conference before the operation, Task Force 57 did its work to my complete satisfaction and fully lived up to the great traditions of the Royal Navy. I remember my Chief of Staff remarking one day during the operation that if Admiral Rawlings and I had known each other for 20 years things could not have gone more smoothly.

During *Iceberg I*, TF-57 carriers had flown 1,961 fighter and 483 Avenger sorties, for a total of 2,444 sorties in 12 days of action. Vian's planes had expended 412 tons of bombs and 315 rockets, claimed 134 total enemy aircraft in the air and on the ground, and sunk or heavily damaged over 100 sampans and small craft. Since leaving Ulithi on 23 March, TF-57 had been replenished at sea with 93,000 tons of bunker oil, 1,300 tons of avgas, a significant amount of stores, 1,064 bags of mail and 43 replacement aircraft from replenishment carriers. TF-57 had lost a combined 68 aircraft and 34 aircrew to combat and operations, while suffering an additional 19 non-flyers killed and 18 badly wounded.

Operation *Iceberg II*, 4 May–25 May 1945

TF-57's second *Iceberg* tour almost never happened. Even as TF-57 was engaging the Japanese in its first *Iceberg* tour, the US chiefs were scheming to re-assign Rawlings' force. By now the Americans had agreed on an invasion of Japan's Home Islands. With the Philippines largely secure, the obvious solution was

Battleships *King George V* and *Howe* bombard Sakashima Gunto airfields and anti-aircraft batteries, 4 May 1945. This would be *Howe*'s only surface shelling in the Pacific theatre, but *King George V* would engage in several bombardments of the Japanese Home Islands. (IWM A 28927)

to re-orient MacArthur's considerable South-West Pacific forces to the north to employ in the invasion of Japan. However, this would leave large Japanese forces in the American rear, particularly North Borneo, which would be invaded by the Australians, with American logistic support. Local naval support, the US chiefs decided, would be provided by the BPF. The US position was to eventually turn this entire backwater over to Mountbatten's South East Asia command by 1 July 1945.

Once again, the Americans appeared to be pushing their British and Commonwealth allies away from the Pacific's decisive theatre. The invasion of Borneo would ultimately take place on 1 May 1945 – but would not include the British Pacific Fleet. By now Nimitz had been fully converted to the value of the British carriers in the front line, and he summarily vetoed any notion of using the BPF anywhere other than with the main US fleet.

Beginning at 0605hrs on 4 May, Rawlings launched two airstrikes totalling 47 Avengers and Fireflies against the Miyako, Ishigaki and Miyara airfields. The strike returned at 0830hrs having lost one Avenger to intense anti-aircraft fire. In response, at 1000hrs Rawling detached most of his surface strength to shell the Sakashima airfields, believing his heavy guns might better crater the airfields and suppress Japanese anti-aircraft batteries. Rawlings also hoped to lift the morale of his bored battleship and cruiser crews. Assigned their own CAP, battleships *King George V* and *Howe*, all five cruisers and six destroyers forged ahead of the carriers and at 1205hrs began shelling Japanese positions at Hirara

SHELLING SAKASHIMA GUNTO, 4 MAY 1945 (overleaf)

On 4 May 1945, Rawlings detached a major surface force to shell the Sakashima Gunto airbases. Rawlings believed heavy battleship and cruiser gunfire could more thoroughly suppress the Japanese anti-aircraft batteries. The force detached from the carriers at 1000hrs. Commanded directly by Rawlings, it included battleships *King George V* and *Howe*, Minotaur-class light cruiser HMS *Swiftsure*, Dido-class light cruisers HMS *Black Prince* and HMS *Euryalus*, Fiji-class cruisers HMCS *Uganda* and HMNZS *Gambia*, and the six destroyers of the 25th Destroyer Flotilla: HMS *Grenville*, HMS *Ursa*, HMS *Undine*, HMS *Urchin*, HMS *Urania* and HMS *Undaunted*. The force was provided with its own fighter CAP, as well as designated fighters for shell spotting.

The force was in position at 1155hrs and commenced the shelling at 1205hrs. The battleships opened fire on Hirara and Nobara airfields at 25,000 yards, while the cruisers

opened up from between 17,000 and 18,000 yards. *King George V* and *Howe* combined to unload 195 14in shells and 378 5.25in shells at the enemy installations. The five cruisers expended 598 6in and 378 5.25in rounds in total.

This scene focuses on the two Fiji-class cruisers, the Royal Canadian Navy's HMCS *Uganda* and the Royal New Zealand Navy's HMNZS *Gambia*. The two cruisers have their 6in turrets swung out to broadside and are bombarding from about 15,000 yards range. They are cruising at about 15 knots.

Almost immediately, Rawlings became aware that kamikazes had crashed two of his carriers over the horizon. Visibly upset, Rawlings did not abort the shelling but ordered his ships to complete the mission as quickly as possible. At 1247hrs the surface force retired back towards the carriers at 25 knots.

and Nobara airfields. Only eight destroyers were left to defend the four carriers. As Vian later rued, 'I was not sufficiently alive to the effect on our defensive system which would be caused by the temporary absence of the radar sets and anti-aircraft armament of the battleships. The Japanese were.'

At least 26 Japanese planes had sortied from Formosa that morning. At 1102hrs the first of four small groups of aircraft was detected on radar and engaged by the CAP. This proved the beginning of a skilful and successful decoy operation by the Japanese. At 1131hrs several undetected aircraft suddenly tore through the 3,000ft overcast and TF-57's gutted anti-aircraft screen. A single Zero strafed the wildly manoeuvring *Formidable* before making a second attack run. Blazing from anti-aircraft fire, it successfully dived into *Formidable*'s flight deck, releasing a 551lb bomb just before impact. The explosion tore a 2ft hole in the flight deck, started fires topside that destroyed 11 parked aircraft, threw splinters almost through the ship that damaged the centre boiler room, and knocked out all but one radar. *Formidable* suffered nine killed and 47 wounded.

Minutes later, a second Zero, ablaze and diving steeply at the hard-turning *Indomitable*, suddenly levelled off at the last moment as if making a touch-and-go, essentially pancaking onto *Indomitable*'s flight deck and clattering over the side before its bomb detonated harmlessly, damaging a radar aerial. Scanning the skies aboard *Indomitable*, Vian was unaware his flagship had even been hit. Seven minutes later, *Indomitable* was attacked by a second blazing suicider that slammed into the ocean ten yards off the starboard bow. Although *Indomitable*'s damage appeared superficial, Vian considered the radar damage serious, as it was the carriers' only SM-1 model, an American height-finding type greatly superior to its British counterparts.

Rawlings' surface force re-united with Vian's carriers at 1420hrs, even as Japanese raids continued. At 1515hrs, a TF-57 Corsair shot down a D4Y Judy dive-bomber, making Lieutenant D. J. Sheppard the Royal Navy's first Pacific fighter ace. TF-57 had shot down 13 enemy aircraft on 4 May, including 11 by fighters and two by anti-aircraft fire, but had lost 13 planes of its own, including the 11 aboard *Formidable*. The 3–4 May *Kikisui* mass attack across Fifth Fleet had ultimately killed 589 British and American sailors, the most Allied naval fatalities of any two-day period during *Iceberg*.

Formidable was badly damaged, but not critically so. By 1254hrs the fires had been doused and the carrier was making 24 knots. The dent in *Formidable*'s armoured flight deck was filled with steel plate and quick-drying cement and at 1700hrs the carrier recovered 13 Corsairs. By 0420hrs the following morning, 5 May, *Formidable* was making full speed. A few hours later two *Formidable* Corsairs, flying refugee-style out of *Victorious*, were vectored against a distant and shortly fleeing high-altitude snooper. The dogged, extremely long-range, high-altitude pursuit finally culminated at 30,000ft with a shot-down Zero. *Victorious* duly complimented those 'paying guests from *Formidable*' and even Vian signalled, 'Nice splash!'

British carrier strikes on 5 May saw no flak whatsoever at Miyako, a credit to the previous day's shelling. Strike results were modest, and three aircraft were lost to accidents. TF-57 replenished over 6–7 May, transferring casualties and polishing repairs to the carriers. Finishing replenishment operations on time, on 7 May Rawlings turned back for the next round of strikes.

Rawlings was inspired to plan another shelling for 8 May, this time keeping two 5.25in-gunned anti-aircraft cruisers with the carriers and keeping the carriers closer to the surface detachment. However, the CAPs were launched in thick murk and heavy rain, inspiring Rawlings to cancel the day's shelling and strikes. Nevertheless, the CAPs remained aloft all day, with the carriers having to employ searchlights to guide their CAP home before retiring overnight.

By morning on 9 May the weather had much cleared and TF-57 launched the standard two strikes against each island. Results were blandly successful as usual, but this time the airfield CAP spied a Val dive-bomber hidden inside a secret cave. The CAP responded by flying low-level attack runs directly at the cave entrance, shooting tracers into the cave that destroyed the Val and left the cave blazing.

At 1645hrs on 9 May, four nearly sea-level bogies were detected approaching at 22nm. The Seafire CAP shot down one, but a single Japanese plane snuck through to successfully crash into *Victorious*, its bomb exploding. Moderate damage was caused to the flight deck, catapult, lift and a 4.5in gun. Moments later, a second attacker dived on the heeling *Victorious*. Hit repeatedly, the kamikaze slammed into *Victorious*'s after flight deck before bouncing into the sea 200 yards abeam. Four parked Corsairs were wrecked but otherwise no significant damage was taken. Within seconds a third kamikaze dived on *Victorious* before suddenly swerving towards *Howe*. The battleship hit the attacker repeatedly, which careered harmlessly overhead and crashed 100 yards away. *Victorious*'s Captain Denny admittedly found kamikaze tactics extremely clever and effective, calling it 'a first-class show from an enemy point of view'.

HMS *Formidable* burns furiously after taking a direct hit on the flight deck on 4 May 1945. *Formidable* suffered eight men dead and 47 wounded in arguably the worst single kamikaze crash the British Pacific Fleet suffered during the war. (IWM A 29717)

Finally, at 1705hrs a fourth attacker made successive runs at *Formidable* and *Indomitable*, both manoeuvring hard and blazing anti-aircraft fire. The kamikaze suddenly turned back and crashed into *Formidable*, which erupted in a huge explosion. The ensuing fire destroyed 18 parked Corsairs but did not greatly endanger *Formidable*, which resumed limited air operations within an hour.

The day's kamikaze strikes had inflicted four killed and 24 injured on *Victorious*, while *Formidable* had lost one dead and eight wounded. Operationally, *Formidable* was down to 11 Corsairs and four Avengers, while *Victorious* had just 28 Corsairs remaining, which could only be operated with difficulty because of the flight deck damage.

With much of his striking power gutted, Rawlings withdrew to an early refuelling rendezvous. During the subsequent 10–11 May replenishment TF-57 made more extensive repairs to the carriers and restocked the depleted air groups. Early on 12 May Rawlings dispatched four radar picket destroyers in a fan formation 12nm out from TF-57. The 5.25in-gunned cruisers were moved in towards the carriers, and each carrier received a 'goalkeeper' anti-kamikaze destroyer immediately astern.

Rawlings then launched the usual strikes against each Sakashima airfield, which successfully re-cratered them at the price of three aircraft and one pilot. According to one historian, 'It was like painting the Forth Bridge, but at least while the daily strikes continued the enemy could not stage planes through, no matter how diligently he repaired them overnight.'

Another four strikes were launched on 13 May, again without Japanese aerial interference. Runways, barracks, storage areas and barges were all shot up and bombed. The daily monotony was broken by the BPF's first submarine alert. A possible contact was detected near the fleet at 0948hrs, triggering a submarine patrol of four Corsairs and three destroyers. Depth charges were fired at 1203hrs, but no substantial contact was made.

The subsequent 14–15 May replenishment was notable for its ammunition transfer. Fifty 1,600lb bombs were transferred via jackstay from *Formidable* to *Black Prince* and then from *Black Prince* to *Indefatigable*. By 0540hrs on 16 May,

A Grumman Avenger of 857 NAS returns from a strike against the Sakashimas, May 1945. The unique British Pacific Fleet roundels are prominently displayed. Beneath the Avenger is its home carrier HMS *Indomitable*. (IWM A 29317)

TF-57 was back off the Sakashimas and launching the first of five strikes. Ninety tons of bombs undid the runway repairs, two lorries full of Japanese soldiers were destroyed and rockets destroyed or damaged ten small vessels. Two *Ohka* suicide rockets were destroyed on the ground, and an inadvertent bomb and huge explosion in the town of Ohama revealed a secret munitions stash. Seven Japanese aircraft were destroyed but TF-57 lost five of their own, although just one was in combat. Late that night submarine USS *Bluefish* rescued a Corsair pilot three miles off Miyako.

British Pacific Fleet Avengers deliver 500lb bombs onto a Sakashima airstrip, 24 May 1945. Bomb craters proved disappointingly fixable, as Task Force 57 would wreck the Sakashima runways every day and the Japanese would re-fill them beneath floodlights every night. The daily air superiority missions nevertheless kept Sakashima air power relatively suppressed. (IWM A 29324)

The following day, 17 May, saw the beginning of terminal bad luck. *Indomitable*'s speed was limited by mechanical problems, while crash-landings aboard *Victorious* killed one, wrecked four planes and damaged landing equipment so thoroughly as to limit air operations. TF-57 managed three underwhelming Avenger strikes before retiring for an 18–19 May refuelling.

During the 18 May replenishment, seven out of 22 planes crashed on landing or take off from escort carrier *Ruler*, killing four airmen. Then at 1100hrs the guns of a *Formidable* Corsair were accidentally fired into an Avenger, which exploded. *Formidable*'s resulting hangar fire caused severe damage, wrecked 30 planes and further crippled *Formidable*'s ability to launch large strikes.

As TF-57 manoeuvred back into launch position early on 20 May, a thick fog descended and destroyer *Quilliam* rammed *Indomitable* from astern. No casualties were reported, but *Quilliam* was badly damaged and ultimately taken under tow by *Black Prince*. Despite the weather, TF-57 attacked Miyako and Ishigaki, albeit with underwhelming results. The following day TF-57 managed five strikes against the islands, but heavy cloud cover again made attack assessments difficult. CAP Hellcats splashed two snoopers near the task force.

TF-57 reached Replenishment Area Cootie at 0700hrs on 22 May, to be reinforced by cruiser *Achilles*. Late that evening *Formidable* detached from TF-57 and withdrew for repairs at Sydney, escorted by destroyers *Kempenfelt* and *Whirlwind*. Likewise, the damaged *Quilliam* was ultimately towed back to Leyte-Samar by the tug USS *Turkey*, escorted by *Black Prince*, escort carrier *Ruler*, and destroyers *Grenville* and *Norman*. The bad news continued the following day when *Ruler* lost two Hellcats and their pilots and *Indomitable* was limited to 22 knots by a malfunctioning shaft.

Now down to three battered carriers, at dawn on 24 May TF-57 resumed Sakashima strikes through drizzly weather. Three strikes armed with 1,600lb bombs significantly cratered Sakashima runways, without loss. The following day TF-57 launched three strikes against Miyako and one against Ishigaki, scoring 48 bomb hits against assigned targets. Photo-reconnaissance revealed an apparent suicide boat base, which was ravaged by rocket-armed Fireflies. Late that evening submarine USS *Bluefish* surfaced to observe engineers repairing the Ishigaki strip under floodlights. *Bluefish* shelled the operation with the deck guns and then withdrew.

Rawlings also retired from the Sakashimas late on 25 May, having fulfilled the Royal Navy's *Iceberg* mission. On 27 May, Rawlings received the following message from Spruance:

> On completion of your two months' operations as a Task Force of the Fifth Fleet in support of the capture of Okinawa, I wish to express to you and to the officers and men under your command, my appreciation of the fine work you have done and the splendid spirit of co-operation in which you have done it. To the American portion of the Fifth Fleet, Task Force 57 has typified the great traditions of the Royal Navy. Signed Spruance.

US forces finally secured Okinawa in late June 1945, successfully concluding Operation *Iceberg*. When TF-57's two *Iceberg* tours are combined, TF-57 had been at sea 62 straight days (eight at Leyte-Samar) and flown 4,893 total sorties, including 2,073 strike sorties that dumped 958 tons of bombs on Japanese facilities and fired 950 3in rockets into enemy targets. TF-57's total aircraft losses came to 160 planes. Of these, 72 were operational losses, including 61 that were Seafire landing accidents. Kamikaze crashes had destroyed 32 total planes on TF-57 carrier decks, while *Formidable*'s unfortunate hangar fire had destroyed another 30. Only 26 TF-57 aircraft had been shot down in combat. Compared to the USN's staggering *Iceberg* losses of 4,907 dead, TF-57 had suffered only 126 total casualties. Of these, 85 were killed or missing, including 41 aircrew.

Task Force 57 flagship *King George V* at Guam, May 1945. Guam was now the forward headquarters for the US Pacific Fleet. Vice Admiral Rawlings took *King George V* to Guam immediately after Task Force 57's final *Iceberg* tour to report in person to Admiral Nimitz. (IWM A 29259)

According to *Victorious*'s Commander R. C. Hay:

> For the first time in five years a British fleet was able to force its will on an enemy air force, but the spectres of Greece and Crete tended still to veil the fact that by 1945 the ships and planes of Task Force 57 were quite capable of taking on an island the size of Formosa – and could do so successfully. For the first time we had the strength, power, and equipment to do this.

Spruance agreed, and in his official report he recommended that in their next operation the British carriers be directly integrated with the US Fast Carrier Task Force.

Undersea Warfare

On 7 June 1945, IJN heavy cruiser *Ashigara* sortied from Batavia in the Japanese-occupied Netherlands East Indies. Escorted by destroyer *Kamikaze*, the heavy cruiser was carrying 1,600 troops and 480 tons of supplies to reinforce the Singapore garrison. Submarine USS *Blueback* spotted the ships and made a contact report, which reached Commander Arthur Hezlet's submarine HMS *Trenchant* accompanied by Lieutenant G. C. Clarabut's submarine HMS *Stygian*. The two submarines took up positions on either side of the Bangka Strait approaches.

Beginning at 0432hrs on 8 June, *Trenchant* and *Kamikaze* briefly spotted each other and exchanged fire. Six hours later, a submerged *Stygian* fired two torpedoes at *Kamikaze*, which counterattacked unsuccessfully with depth charges. Then at 1148hrs *Trenchant* spotted *Ashigara* and at 1208hrs launched a salvo of eight torpedoes at the Japanese heavy cruiser at a range of 4,700 yards. Five torpedoes struck *Ashigara*, causing severe damage and a spreading fire. The crippled heavy cruiser then opened fire at *Trenchant*'s periscope; *Trenchant* responded by firing two stern torpedoes which missed. *Ashigara* capsized at 1239hrs, with both British submarines ultimately escaping. Although over 800 of *Ashigara*'s crew were rescued, at least 1,200 Japanese troops went down with the cruiser.

In July 1945 BPF submarines undertook two separate wire-cutting operations. In Operation *Sable*, submarine HMS *Spearhead* towed XE craft *XE4* to within 40nm of the Mekong Delta. Operating from the submerged *XE4*, two divers successfully located and manually cut two Hong Kong–Saigon submarine telephone cables. The second mission, Operation *Foil*, saw

A British Pacific Fleet XE craft underway at Sydney. In early 1945 the BPF arranged a demonstration of the XE craft at Pearl Harbor. The Americans were unenthusiastic, believing midget submarines were unnecessarily suicidal, and also because XE craft looked suspiciously like weapons to employ against Japanese capital ships. (Bettmann/Getty Images)

submarine HMS *Selene* tow *XE5* close to Hong Kong, where divers cut the Hong Kong–Singapore telephone cable with difficulty.

On 1 August 1945 the BPF executed Operation *Struggle*, an attack on the Japanese heavy cruisers *Myoko* and *Takao* off Singapore. For 11 hours, submarines HMS *Spark* and HMS *Stygian* crept along the Johore Strait, towing *XE1* and *XE3* respectively.

Two hours after *Stygian* released *XE3*, the midget sub's diver attached two 2-ton naval mines to *Takao*. By now *XE3*'s companion, *XE1*, realized its assigned target *Myoko* was too far away, and therefore *XE1* now also attached its mines to *Takao*, and both XE craft successfully escaped. The detonating charges wrecked *Takao*, causing the heavy cruiser to settle on the seafloor of the shallow strait. *XE3*'s commander and diver were both awarded the Victoria Cross.

Operation *Inmate*, 14 June 1945

By 8 May, fleet carrier *Implacable* had reached Sydney from Britain. *Implacable* was scheduled to join Vian's carrier force during the coming July campaign. Rawlings directed *Implacable* and other newly arrived BPF warships to conduct a practice raid against the leapfrogged Japanese island base at Truk to gain combat seasoning. Commanded by 4th Cruiser Squadron's Rear Admiral E. J. P. Brind, the formation was designated TG-111.2 and comprised fleet carrier *Implacable*, escort carrier *Ruler*, cruisers *Swiftsure*, *Uganda*, *Achilles* and *Newfoundland*, and the five destroyers of the newly arrived 24th Destroyer Flotilla. Aboard *Implacable* were 80 aircraft, while *Ruler* functioned as a virtually empty emergency flight deck for *Implacable*.

A simultaneous air and surface strike was planned for 14 June, with the four cruisers and destroyers *Troubridge*, *Teazer* and *Tenacious* steaming ahead overnight to be off Truk by dawn. Although weather was good over Truk, it was rainy over the two carriers. Nevertheless, *Implacable* maintained strikes every 2–3 hours from a position 60–80nm off Truk. A US lifeguard submarine was on station to rescue downed flyers, while *Ruler* landed six Seafires aboard that had been unable to find *Implacable* in the weather.

Meanwhile Brind separated his surface force into three units and began a methodical training bombardment of Truk coastal batteries, with *Implacable* stationed 20nm away for close support. Minor return fire was received by the surface ships and silenced. A total of 113 offensive and 110 defensive sorties were launched. These included a night-time strike of six Avengers on

During Operation *Inmate*, on 14 June 1945, 6in shellfire from a British Pacific Fleet light cruiser lands at Truk. The once-formidable Truk had been neutralized by the Americans and bypassed in 1944, making it an ideal target to pummel for a training mission. (IWM A 29462)

14/15 June, a first for the BPF. At dawn TGG-111.2 reassembled and withdrew, reaching Manus on 17 June. No planes or crew had been lost.

The Naval Siege of Japan, 16 July–14 August 1945

Admiral Bill Halsey had taken over command of US Fifth Fleet from Spruance on 27 May. Fifth Fleet was accordingly re-designated Third Fleet, meaning Rawlings' TF-57 was reflagged as TF-37. Rawlings' US Fast Carrier counterpart, Mitscher's TF-58, was also reflagged as TF-38 and now commanded by Vice Admiral John McCain. Battleship *Howe* was being refitted in Durban, leaving *King George V* as TF-37's only battleship. Additionally, carrier *Indomitable* also was being overhauled in Sydney, leaving TF-37 with the standard four fleet carriers.

Exactly how to force Japan's unconditional surrender had long been controversial. But on 25 May 1945 the US high command authorized Operation *Downfall*, the invasion of the Japanese homeland. *Downfall*'s first phase would be the invasion of southern Kyushu, scheduled for 1 November 1945 (X-Day) and codenamed Operation *Olympic*. From southern Kyushu, US forces would then launch the decisive invasion into central Honshu and conquer Tokyo. This massive *coup de grâce* was codenamed Operation *Coronet* and was scheduled for 1 March 1946.

Nimitz's huge and still growing Fifth/Third Fleet (including its incorporated BPF) would finally be divided into two separate and simultaneous fleets for the invasion of Japan. For the first time, Spruance and Halsey would command concurrently. Staging from the Philippines, the Marianas and Okinawa, Spruance's Fifth Fleet would 'conduct the operations connected with the seizure and occupation of beachheads in southern Kyushu'. Halsey's Third Fleet, operating out of Eniwetok, would 'provide strategic support by raiding Honshu and Hokkaido'.

As part of the *Olympic* preliminaries, Halsey's Third Fleet was tasked with softening-up the Home Islands. These operations would begin in July 1945 and include TF-37. After hammering Japan for a month, Halsey would retire in mid-August to replenish at forward bases. Third Fleet would then sortie again in late

A *Formidable* cameraman captures trailing carriers *Implacable* and *Illustrious* and their escorting destroyers on 10 July 1945. Now designated Task Force 37, the carrier strike force is en route to meet Halsey's US Third Fleet to begin British naval strikes on the Home Islands. (IWM A 30192)

August and resume strikes against the Home Islands. At this point, Rawlings' TF-37 would be reinforced to nine carriers by the light carriers of the 11th Aircraft Carrier Squadron (11 ACS). TF-37 would then temporarily detach from Third Fleet to launch diversionary strikes against Hong Kong on 18 September and Canton on 28 September. By December 1945, six refurbished carriers would return to the combat zone, including fast carriers *Victorious* and *Illustrious*. Accompanying them would be a seventh carrier, the brand-new Canadian light carrier *Ocean*.

Beginning in July 1945, TF-37 would operate directly with the US fast carriers for the first time. This was partly thanks to Spruance, who in his post-*Iceberg* report had acknowledged to Nimitz that the British carriers were now ready to operate with the US Fast Carrier Task Force.

TF-37 reached Manus on 4 July, prompting Rawlings to signal Halsey: 'I hereby report TF-37 for duty with Third Fleet. We are much looking forward to this, our first operation under your orders.' Halsey responded: 'Your 040023Z acknowledged with pleasure. Please be prepared to board *Missouri* by British destroyer at first rendezvous for operations conference. CTF 38 [McCain] will attend and I suggest you bring officers qualified to discuss detailed air plans.'

The southern and central Home Islands had been under sustained US strategic bombing since November 1944. However, northern Japan remained untouched, as it lay outside the safe range of Marianas-based B-29s. Although Halsey had free rein against Japan's entire coastline, it was essential northern Japan be brought under attack. Much of Halsey's summer campaign would be spent rectifying this issue.

Halsey described:

> We sortied from Leyte under a broad directive: we would attack the enemy's home islands, destroy the remnants of his navy, merchant marine, and air power, and cripple his factories and communications. Our planes would strike inland; our big guns would bombard coastal targets; together they would literally bring the war home to the average Japanese citizen.

US intelligence estimated that as many as 5,000 kamikazes would assault the *Olympic* invasion fleet. The USN's top priority was now to locate and destroy the dispersed aircraft at Kyushu's estimated 60+ airfields.

On 15 July battleship *King George V* somewhat desperately improvised an abeam fuelling method with tanker *Dingledale* that was surprisingly successful. Afterwards all BPF capital ships would refuel using the more efficient abeam method.

Halsey's Third Fleet had already launched three days of air and surface strikes against central and northern Honshu. Early on 16 July, Third Fleet retired to a position east of Honshu to replenish. Halsey's fast carrier force TF-38 and Rawlings' already-refuelled TF-37 rendezvoused at dawn. From now on Third Fleet would always include a British contingent. Rawlings, Vian and their staffs transferred to Halsey's flagship *Missouri* to conference. Halsey provided Rawlings with three possible alternatives:

1. TF-37 would operate close aboard, as another task group in TF-38; it would not receive direct orders from me, but would be privy to the orders that I gave TF-38; these it would consider as 'suggestions' to be followed to our mutual advantage, thereby assuring us a concentrated force with concentrated weapons.
2. TF-37 would operate semi-independently, some 60–70 miles away, thereby preserving its tactical identity at the cost of a divided force. I stipulated that I would consent to this only if the request were put in writing.
3. TF-37 would operate completely independently, against soft spots in Japan which we would recommend if so desired.

According to Halsey: 'Admiral Rawlings did not hesitate. He said "Of course I'll accept Number 1." My admiration for him began at that moment. I saw him constantly thereafter, and a finer officer and a firmer friend I have never known.'

Rawlings later explained, 'The principal points, which were settled forthwith, were the desire of the British task force to work in close tactical co-operation with TF-38, conforming to their movements, and that we should take part in battleship and cruiser bombardments as well as in surface sweeps.'

By 1600hrs the new Anglo-American fleet was heading back towards Japan at 15 knots, with Halsey filling his Third Fleet radar picket stations with destroyers regardless of their nationality. Rawlings reflected: 'The Allied Fleets were at last in close proximity under the same Commander' and that the event might 'prove a not unimportant milestone on the long road of the world's history'.

Seafires of *Implacable*'s 880 NAS roar over Japan's Chiba Prefecture, 17 July 1945. They have just become the first British aircraft to penetrate Home Island airspace. However, encroaching fog would require them to abort their mission early. (IWM A 29964)

The augmented naval force closing in on the Home Islands was staggering indeed. McCain's TF-38 comprised ten heavy and six light American fast carriers, totalling 1,190 planes. Rawlings' four heavy fast carriers brought another 255 planes, for a new Third Fleet total of 20 fast carriers and 1,445 aircraft. The carriers and their aircraft were escorted by a total of nine Allied battleships, 25 cruisers and 81 destroyers.

At 0350hrs on 17 July, Third Fleet began launching airstrikes against central Honshu. In this final month of World War II, Halsey's Third Fleet would fly over 11,000 offensive sorties against the Home Islands. However, on this day weather was poor, and the Americans' TF-38 only flew 205 strike sorties, with only 56 planes being able to bomb through the overcast. Rawlings' TF-37 launched its strikes against north-west Honshu, with the British flying 78 offensive sorties in the Royal Navy's first-ever airstrike against Japan. British aircraft hit four Japanese airfields at Masuda, Niigata, Sendai and Matsushima, expending 83 500lb bombs and 26 rockets. TF-37 airmen claimed nine Japanese aircraft, a hangar and three locomotives destroyed, plus one junk sunk off the coast. A similar score was believed damaged. Five British aircraft and two aircrew were lost.

In stark contrast to *Iceberg*, TF-37 planes encountered zero Japanese aerial resistance. Nor did any Japanese air raids appear to counterattack. Even Japanese reconnaissance patrols and snoopers appeared to be permanently grounded. Clearly a new Japanese strategy was at hand. Indeed, since late March the IJNAF and IJAAF had lost 3,000 aircraft (including 1,465 kamikazes) off Okinawa and the Sakashima Gunto. With an invasion of Japan quite obviously the next Allied move, in July the Japanese high command had chosen to radically conserve its kamikaze forces for the seemingly imminent landings. Japanese aircraft were accordingly defueled, dispersed and camouflaged, often miles from their runways. The situation is best described by a US report from 10 July:

> No aerial opposition was encountered although several of our planes were damaged by anti-aircraft. Our pilots discovered that the Japs were playing it very cagey with their air force. Planes were cunningly camouflaged and hidden in dispersal areas and covered revetments sometimes as far as two miles from the field itself. Hunting out and destroying such planes was a primary mission of the squadron and a tough one, in the face of the enemy's concentration of anti-aircraft fire.

Third Fleet had already made the first two battleship bombardments of Japan, with three of Halsey's fast battleships shelling Honshu's Kamaishi steelworks on 14 July, and three additional fast battleships (including Halsey's flagship *Missouri*) shelling industrial targets at Muroran, Hokkaido, a major coal, coke and pig iron production centre. Both bombardments had been conducted in broad daylight. Halsey explained that the purpose of his surface shelling missions was 'to destroy industries, demoralize transportation, and lower the will to resist of the Japanese people'.

On 17 July Halsey detached a third US surface force of five fast battleships, two light cruisers and eight destroyers under Rear Admiral Oscar Badger (USN) to ravage the Americans' latest strategic target. Halsey again rode along aboard *Missouri*, but this time the Americans would be accompanied by a British delegation, detached from TF-37's main force at 1430hrs. The British formation comprised battleship *King George V* and escorting destroyers *Quality* and *Quiberon*. Like Halsey, Rawlings joined his flagship. Rawlings' detachment shortly joined with Badger's force, with the combined flotilla designated TU-34.8.2. The target was the industrial city of Hitachi, population 85,000. Located some 80nm north-east of Tokyo, Hitachi boasted copper mines and was a major electronics-producing centre.

Third Fleet's designated night carrier, USS *Bonhomme Richard* (CV-31), provided the overhead CAP in the form of radar-equipped F6F-5N Hellcat night fighters. The six Allied battleships assembled in column, with Badger's five battleships in the van and *King George V* bringing up the rear. Visibility that night was just three miles, forcing the Allies to navigate by radar and soundings. Shrouded by fog and rain, the Allied battleships opened fire on Hitachi at 2314hrs, 17 July. There was no opposition from the Japanese, and the Allies suffered no damage in their single pass.

Over the course of 53 minutes, the combined six battleships pummelled Hitachi and Mito with a total of 1,805 heavy battery shells (representing 2,000 tons of ordnance) in the war's largest surface bombardment of the Japanese homeland. *King George V* unleashed a total of 297 14in rounds at Japanese targets ashore, including 91 rounds at the Densen engineering works, 79 rounds at the Taga engineering works and another 97 shells at an unidentified industrial complex.

At 0007hrs on 18 July, all Allied ships ceased fire and withdrew. The battleships had struck three major target areas, the Taga Works and Mito Works of the Hitachi Manufacturing Company, the Yamate Plant of the Hitachi Works of the Hitachi Manufacturing Company, and the copper refining section of the Hitachi mines.

Not surprisingly, some built-up urban areas were also hit by accident, damaging housing and public utilities. Later analysis would reveal that the direct physical damage to the industrial installations was less than desired. Nevertheless, battleship shellings proved much more damaging psychologically than any air attack, wrecking civilian morale and causing severe worker absenteeism. Thousands of Japanese civilians fled Hitachi for the countryside the following morning.

Planes from *Victorious*, *Implacable* and *Formidable* bomb Shikoku's Takamatsu Airfield, 24 July 1945. The British aircraft have intentionally been routed away from Kure to save the Japanese capital ships for the Americans alone. (IWM A 29961)

According to Halsey, 'These sweeps and bombardments accomplished more than destruction. They showed the enemy that we made no bones about playing in his front yard. From now on, we patrolled his channels and shelled his coast almost every night that the weather permitted.'

Halsey knew that Rawlings' ships had less fuel capacity and were slower refuelling than the Americans and had planned for TF-37 to conduct strike operations for only two days out of Halsey's planned three-day strike periods. However, when Rawlings' ships were allowed to refuel from US oilers, Halsey found that TF-37 'was able to match us strike for strike'.

The US naval high command had become irrationally obsessed with putting every Japanese capital ship on the bottom. After the battleship *Nagato* was discovered camouflaged at Yokosuka, Halsey dedicated five US fleet carriers to destroying it. Third Fleet duly launched airstrikes against the Tokyo area on 18 July. Although hampered by weather, TF-37 launched 58 strike sorties, which attacked a seaplane base at Kitaura and airfields at Nobara, Naruto, Chosi, Kanoike, Natori and Kitakawa. However, saltwater had contaminated *Victorious*'s fuel bunkers, limiting the carrier to launching just six Corsairs. TF-37 and TF-38 claimed a combined 43 enemy planes destroyed on the ground and 77 planes damaged but lost a combined 14 planes and 18 aircrew to fierce anti-aircraft fire. That evening TF-37 and TF-38 retired towards their refuelling rendezvous. Overconsumption by *Indefatigable*'s group had left the LSG tankers 2,000 tons short of fuel during the 20 July replenishment. Rawlings was forced to ask Halsey if *Uganda*, *Gambia* and *Newfoundland* could refuel from US oilers, which Halsey readily allowed. Ordered by Nimitz, Halsey now prepared to attack Japan's last surviving battleships and carriers at Kure.

The three days of strikes that began on 24 July remain controversial, for two separate reasons. Firstly, the IJN's dilapidated capital ships were known to be uselessly trapped in harbour and already of virtually no military value; even the majority of TF-38 brass opposed the attack. The second source of controversy is for the undeniably petty way the USN treated the BPF during the episode, in stark contrast to the two organizations' relationship during the rest of the war. Between 24 and 28 July, Third Fleet hammered the Inland Sea area, with Halsey's TF-38 focusing on sinking the remnants of the IJN combined fleet immobilized and useless at Kure. While the Americans focused on the most heavily defended location in the world, Rawlings' planes were routed to secondary targets.

In his post-war memoirs, Halsey explained that 'it was imperative that we forestall a possible post-war claim by Britain that she had delivered even a part of the final blow that demolished the Japanese Fleet'. This statement is glaringly out-of-character for Halsey, considering his magnanimous command and commentary of TF-57, even in the same memoirs. However, Halsey's stated sentiment was certainly in line with Nimitz and the USN high command in general. One suspects the post-war Halsey was covering for his old bosses.

On 24 July, TF-37 flew 257 sorties against targets in Japan or just offshore, doing considerable damage. Vian reported that *Victorious*'s Lieutenant-Commander J. C. N. Shrubsole led a force that 'ranged the whole north shore of the Inland Sea, visiting airfield after airfield, leaving a trail of wrecked buildings and burning enemy planes'. Another strike, led by Lieutenant-Commander A. J. Griffith, ran into foul weather and became scattered. Despite only managing to assemble six Avengers, two Corsairs and two Fireflies, the *Victorious* flyers discovered the escort carrier *Shimane Maru* hiding at Shido Bay. Fierce rocket and bomb attacks ensured *Shimane Maru* the honour of being the first carrier ever sunk by a British carrier.

Night-trained hecklers from TF-38 harassed Kure overnight, keeping Kure gunners awake. TF-37 resumed its strikes at 0430hrs, launching 155 strike sorties on 25 July before deteriorating weather forced strikes to be suspended. That evening, BPF Hellcats shot down three Japanese torpedo planes. The BPF had lost one Avenger for the day.

TF-37 and TF-38 retired to replenish. Together they had launched a total of 2,589 Allied strike sorties since the morning of 24 July. At dawn the next morning TF-38 and TF-37 rendezvoused with their respective replenishment groups. In a small 26 July experiment, supply ship *Robert Maersk* successfully transferred a

KING GEORGE V SHELLS HAMAMATSU, MIDNIGHT 29/30 JULY, 1945 (overleaf)

The 14in guns of *King George V* fire broadsides at industrial targets in Hamamatsu. As part of the combined Allied column, *King George V* made two passes against Hamamatsu. According to the post-action reports, the bombarding Allied ships enjoyed a clear night sky, with bright moonlight and good visibility. *King George V* would unleash 265 14in shells at the Japanese Musical Instrument Company, causing fires that were 'pleasingly visible from the ship'. Incidentally, the Hamamatsu bombardment proved to be the last time the main battery of a British ship-of-the-line was ever fired in anger.

The post-war United States Strategic Bombing Survey (USSBS) established that at least six 14in shells fell within the boundaries of the Japan Musical Instrument Company's Tenryu plant, including four within the built-up area. *King George V* scored direct hits on the Tenryu plant's Buildings No. 9 and No. 25, along with a log conveyer. The fourth shell scored a near miss between Buildings No. 22 and No. 24. A total of 6,600 square feet of floor space suffered structural damage from *King George V*'s gunfire.

The post-war USSBS discovered a curious aspect of battleship bombardments against industrial targets. According to the USSBS:

'Inasmuch as the most important of [the Japan Musical Instrument Company's] propeller production facilities (which had already survived the numerous air attacks against Hamamatsu without severe damage) again escaped serious injury in naval surface bombardment, direct effects of attack upon its production were negligible. However, indirect effects of gunfire (e.g. labour absentee-ism and idleness, disruption of utilities, etc.) caused a total stoppage of production (which had already fallen to about three per cent of peak production) and prompted abandonment of all efforts to produce propellers at this plant.'

As the Anglo-American surface force withdrew, flagship *South Dakota* signalled, 'Well done to all hands. Let's do it again. Signed RAdm Shafroth.'

small amount of ordnance to *King George V* while underway, a first for a British battleship. The following day *Robert Maersk* transferred a substantially larger amount to *King George V*, while *Glenartney* provisioned *Indefatigable*, *Formidable* and three cruisers.

One of the BPF's more unpleasant incidents reached its conclusion during the at-sea replenishment on 27 July, during the middle of the 24–28 July Inland Sea strikes. Aside from North American operations and the doomed 1941 Hong Kong defence, the Canadian-manned cruiser HMCS *Uganda*, then attached to TF-37, had provided Canada's only wartime military deployment in the Pacific War.

However, Canadian public support for the war effort had never been as intense as that in Britain or the United States, nations which had suffered direct attacks from major Axis forces. On 4 April 1945, the Canadian government had ruled that all Pacific-bound men would have to re-volunteer. For many Canadian volunteers, there was an additional belief that their 'duration of the hostilities' enlistment terms referred to Germany, not Japan. A 7 May referendum saw 605 of *Uganda*'s 907 Canadian crewmen vote against continuing the war. This was a substantially legal move, and therefore not truly a mutiny. Nevertheless, *Uganda* continued to serve with TF-37 until an enraged Admiralty could replace the cruiser with *Argonaut*. In a move deeply resented among the British and American rank-and-file, on 27 July HMCS *Uganda* detached from TF-37 to return to Esquimalt, British Columbia, via Eniwetok and Pearl Harbor. Canadians continued to be represented in the BPF, but as individuals. The BPF's next Canadian warship, auxiliary cruiser HMCS *Prince Robert*, would only arrive in early August, never seeing action.

The combined task forces completed refuelling the afternoon of 27 July and proceeded back towards Japan. Early the following morning the Allied carriers were 100nm off Shikoku and began launching resumed strikes against the Inland Sea area, as well as airfields on the north-western Honshu coast. TF-37 flew 260 offensive sorties against the eastern Inland Sea, including Avenger strikes at the Harima dockyard and Corsair attacks against Maizuru, sinking or severely damaging several IJN escorts. TF-37's losses came to eight aircraft and two airmen for the day.

After launching 4,292 total offensive sorties at the Inland Sea area since 24 July, at 1930hrs on 28 July, Halsey's Third Fleet began its retirement from the Kure region and steamed for its new launching point for planned strikes against Osaka-Nagoya. The following day, 29 July, Halsey dispatched Rear Admiral Shafroth's US group of three fast battleships, four heavy cruisers and ten destroyers to bombard industrial targets at Hamamatsu. Rendezvousing with the American surface force were *King George V* and destroyers *Undine*, *Ulysses* and *Urania*. The battleship shelling began at 2315hrs on 29 July and lasted one hour and 12 minutes. Unbeknownst to its participants, the Hamamatsu bombardment represented the end of a storied era: just after midnight on

30 July 1945 would be the last time the main guns of a British battleship were ever fired in anger.

Co-ordinating with Halsey's carriers, TF-37 launched 216 strike sorties on 30 July, attacking shipping and hitting airfields in the Maizuru/Nagoya Bay area. British planes sank frigate *Okinawa* and many small coasters, but lost two Seafires and a Corsair, including their pilots. Meanwhile, Halsey continued his relentless high-speed assault on the Japanese. At one point TF-57 fell 60nm behind the onrushing US carriers. Admiral Fraser observed:

> With easy grace [Halsey] is striking here one day and there the next, replenishing at sea as the situation demands. With dogged persistence the British Pacific Fleet is keeping up, and if anything is going to stretch its muscles, these operations will. But it is tied by a string to Australia and much handicapped by its few, small tankers.

Nevertheless, Halsey would be slowed by typhoon weather in the next two weeks, a situation Rawlings and Vian may have secretly welcomed. As August broke, Halsey mysteriously backed away from the Japanese coastline. Then on 4 August, a US staff officer was sent to *King George V* in person to inform Rawlings of the atomic bomb. Two days later the first bomb was detonated on Hiroshima.

Believing his initial 14 July bombardment of the Kamaishi steel mill had been ineffective, Halsey detached Rear Admiral Shafroth's TU-34.8.1 of three battleships, four heavy cruisers and nine destroyers to mount a second shelling. This time they would be accompanied by a British contingent. Unfortunately *King George V* was suffering from machinery problems that prevented the

Japanese auxiliary escort carrier *Shimane Maru* comes under *Victorious* bomb and rocket attack while anchored at Shido Bay, 24 July 1945. The 11,800-ton carrier ultimately broke in half and sank, losing six men killed. (IWM A 29959)

battleship from attaining the minimum speed US planners required for the attack. TF-37's sole battleship was therefore removed from the Kamaishi bombardment mission. Nevertheless, TF-37 was able to contribute with Rear Admiral Brind's TU-37.1.8, comprising cruisers HMS *Newfoundland* and HMNZS *Gambia*, and destroyers HMS *Tenacious*, *Termagant* and *Terpsichore*.

With 20 US fighters flying CAP overhead, the combined force opened fire at 1247hrs on 9 August. When Japanese flak opened on US spotting planes, *Gambia* commenced counter-battery fire against the Japanese anti-aircraft guns. The bombardment force ceased fire at 1445hrs and retired. The combined 14 July and 9 August Third Fleet bombardments of Kamaishi reduced its steel mill to 35 per cent of its initial value, while collateral damage caused fires in town and destroyed much of Kamaishi's fishing industry. Coming hours after the Soviet invasion of Manchuria and the atomic bombing of Nagasaki, the 9 August bombardment would be the last surface shelling of the war.

Meanwhile, Third Fleet carriers were also busy. From a position off north-eastern Honshu, TF-37 launched 237 strike sorties at Japanese airfields and shipping in Onagawa Wan. Some 120 tons of ordnance was expended, the Fleet Air Arm's single-day record in the war. TF-37 scored 50 of the 250 enemy planes claimed destroyed on the ground, while sinking several small auxiliaries.

However, the most notable action was by Lieutenant Robert Hampton Gray, DSC, RCNVR. Gray was leading his Corsair flight in an extremely low-level attack run when he got caught in Japanese crossfire. Although his Corsair was set ablaze, Gray single-mindedly drove home the attack, scoring a direct hit that destroyed escort sloop *Amakusa* even as he fatally crashed into the harbour. Gray was one of seven British aircraft and five airmen lost on 9 August. For his actions Gray was posthumously awarded the Victoria Cross.

The following day Halsey ordered possibly the most destructive airfield attacks of the war. On 10 August TF-37 aircraft worked over even more parked aircraft at previously untouched Honshu airfields, as well as shipping at Maizuru and in the Inland Sea. Total British losses over 9–10 August were 13 aircraft and nine airmen.

Third Fleet was days from retiring for Eniwetok and Manus to rest and replenish for the second and final pre-invasion offensive, but that evening Halsey's flagship *Missouri* intercepted a mysterious transmission suggesting Japan was in negotiations to surrender. The following morning, 11 August, the American and British flagships found themselves refuelling simultaneously from oiler USS *Sabine*. A giddy Halsey couldn't resist the opportunity: 'I went across to the "Cagey Five" as we called her, on an aerial trolley, just to drink a toast with Vice Admiral Rawlings.'

By now it seemed increasingly likely that Japan could collapse within days, and Halsey wished to keep the pressure on. The BPF's supply arrangements had been made under the expectation Third Fleet would retire on 10 August; even the US force was feeling the strain. But for the Royal Navy to have come so far and sacrificed so much only to be absent at the *coup de grâce* was unthinkable. Unable to keep the full TF-37 at sea, Rawlings offered to keep a token force with Halsey, so long that the British could use American logistic services. Halsey and Nimitz agreed. After replenishment, *King George V*, *Indefatigable*, *Gambia*, *Newfoundland* and ten destroyers were re-designated TG-38.5 and subsumed into McCain's TF-38, the only time the BPF was explicitly subordinated to a US commander. Led by Vian, the remainder of TF-37 reluctantly retired for Manus.

A typhoon warning cancelled planned 12 August strikes, but on 13 August the newly combined TF-38 would hurl 1,167 Anglo-American strike sorties against the Tokyo area. Virtually no Japanese fighters rose to intercept. Just seven Allied planes and one pilot were lost, all operationally. As TF-38 refuelled on 14 August, McCain reminded his men, 'This war could last many months longer. We cannot afford to relax. Now is the time to pour it on.'

Victory, 15 August–2 September 1945

The next morning, on 15 August, TF-38 launched its first wave of 103 aircraft. Twelve Zeros intercepted *Indefatigable*'s 18-plane strike. The British shot down eight but lost one Seafire. By 0614hrs the first wave was returning and the second wave minutes from its targets when suddenly Admiral Nimitz, the Pacific commander-in-chief, ordered Halsey: 'Air attack will be suspended. Acknowledge.' At 1100hrs Halsey signalled, 'Cease hostilities.'

Possibly unaware of the ceasefire, a D4Y Suisei suddenly erupted from the clouds and dropped two bombs against *Indefatigable*, which missed. A US

Admiral Sir Bruce Fraser, commander-in-chief British Pacific Fleet, signs the Instrument of Surrender on behalf of the United Kingdom, 2 September 1945. Fraser would later recall the event as the proudest moment of his life. (HMSO/Public Domain)

Corsair shot it down. Halsey ordered, 'Shoot down all snoopers, but in a friendly sort of way.'

Back on 11 November 1918, the Grand Fleet's Admiral Beatty had celebrated the Armistice with Germany by ordering, 'All hands splice mainbrace, except for Squadron Five.' The term 'splice the mainbrace' is an old sailing double entendre meaning to break out the grog. Because alcohol was illegal aboard US warships, Beatty's giddy victory signal had been more than a Fleet-wide acknowledgement of victory; it had also cleverly acknowledged Beatty's appreciation for the US battleship squadron under his command.

Remembering his history, a jubilant Halsey now signalled 'Splice the mainbrace', to his entire Third Fleet. Such an order was still flagrantly illegal aboard the US ships, which Halsey winkingly acknowledged five minutes later when he altered the addressees to 'All Task Group Commanders except those of the American Groups.'

At noon, Japanese national radio broadcast the Emperor's pre-recorded speech announcing that Japan had ceased hostilities. In the typical Japanese fashion, 'surrender' was never explicitly stated, but only implied. Nevertheless, the Japanese people were to cooperate unconditionally with the Allied powers, effective immediately. Yet not all obeyed. Earlier that morning, Seafire pilot Sub-Lieutenant Fred Hockley had been shot down and captured by the IJA. Despite the widely broadcast ceasefire announcement, Hockley was executed that evening.

Occupation and Liberation, August–September 1945

Between 1 July and 15 August 1945, TF-37 had flown 1,172 strike sorties that expended 460 tons of bombs and 56 rockets against Japanese targets. A total of 43 TF-37 aircraft had been lost. Meanwhile, Halsey maintained the usual defensive measures and ordered TF-38 to patrol an area 100–200nm south-east of the Tokyo area. The BPF commander Admiral Fraser was finally able to join his fleet at sea on 18 August. Accompanying Fraser's flagship *Duke of York* were destroyers *Wager* and *Whelp*; together the three ships comprised Fraser's personal TF-113. Upon their arrival, all BPF warships present reorganized into TF-37 and TG-30.2 (British Flagship Group).

The US and British flagship groups entered Tokyo Bay on 29 August, led by Halsey's *Missouri* and Fraser's *Duke of York*. That same morning the first Allied landing parties touched down and began securing the waterfront. Over the next few days several additional BPF ships trickled into Tokyo Bay alongside Halsey's contingent. Rawlings wrote that 'it was, perhaps, rather a small force to represent a large Empire but its ships had seen many oceans and fought several enemies before they joined their Allies in the Pacific'.

The short, melancholy 2 September 1945 surrender ceremony took place aboard battleship *Missouri*. Admiral Fraser signed the instrument of surrender on behalf of the United Kingdom. Keeping his pen, Fraser wrote to Churchill, who responded: 'I am most grateful to you for your very kind letter written on the date and with the pen of the unconditional surrender of Japan … Not once or twice in our rough island story, the path of duty was the path of glory.'

ANALYSIS

Memories of the British Pacific Fleet are often dominated by technological imagery – the frightfulness of the kamikazes, the resilience of armoured flight decks and the unlikely confrontation of two legendary fighters, the Spitfire and the Zero. However, the true story of the British Pacific Fleet is the resourcefulness, resiliency and courage of its officers and enlisted men, who were cast headlong into the raging climax of a war they had never been trained for. Except for the kamikazes, by 1945 the US Navy was fighting its war exactly how it wanted. The same could not be said for the British Pacific Fleet, which was thrown into someone else's fire and forced to adapt to a categorically alien way of fighting. According to Roskill: 'There is no doubt that the staunchness and spirit of the British crews finally won the wholehearted admiration of their Allies, some of whom had been very reluctant to see the White Ensign fighting alongside their own.'

The British Pacific Fleet deserves high marks for its wartime improvisation and its effective relations with Commonwealth allies and especially the USN. The BPF's wartime courage and combat effectiveness did full credit to the Royal Navy's high traditions. On the other hand, British planning in 1944 had simply not counted on such rapid US strategic progress by 1945. Because of this, BPF

The wrecked remains of a log conveyor at Hamamatsu's Japanese Musical Instrument Company, courtesy of a *King George V* 14in shell. This photograph comes from a post-war US government survey commissioned to scientifically analyse Allied bombing of Axis targets. (United States Strategic Bombing Survey)

logistics were always far behind BPF lines. BPF logistics had to be built from scratch and they simply never came close to catching up to what was necessary during the war, and this hobbled the BPF straight through to August 1945. Aside from the disastrous interwar politics that crippled wartime Royal Navy aviation,

Carrier HMS *Victorious* anchored at Noumea, New Caledonia, in 1943 while serving with the US Navy in the South Pacific. Contrary to enduring American myth, *Victorious* was never renamed USS *Robin* – 'Robin' was simply *Victorious*'s radio callsign while serving with the Americans. (Author's collection)

this 'too-far-behind' logistic situation was the BPF's main problem that (with sufficient foresight) could have been done better.

By far the primary criticism of the British Pacific Fleet is simply that it did not arrive in the Pacific sooner. However, this was not the fault of the BPF itself. From January to September 1944 Churchill and his chiefs of staff wasted a staggering eight months arguing over where a British Far East fleet should go, and what it should do. This constituted a critical eight-month period during which virtually no groundwork on a logistical base could be done. Because the chiefs of staff's decision proved quite correct, and because the USN (despite its pretentions) could not realistically block a major British effort against Japan, the blame for this inexcusable delay must fall squarely on Churchill.

The British Pacific Fleet's wartime deployment proved an indirect political boon to the United States. Had the US government publicly rejected Britain's wartime offer of direct combat assistance in the Pacific, the resulting disillusionment on the American home front could have produced serious political consequences. Could the United States have defeated Japan without the British Pacific Fleet? The short answer is yes. But would that victory have been longer and bloodier? Did British and Commonwealth blood and treasure (and armoured decks) indirectly save American lives at British expense? Again, the short answer is yes. If the Pacific War is viewed as the international effort it was, then BPF involvement in the Pacific was necessary and correct.

But most importantly, Japan's 1941–42 conquest of the British Far East was tantamount to a tragic, multinational catastrophe. So long as Japan's fanatical warlords remained unbowed on their Home Islands, millions of Commonwealth civilians and nearly 200,000 prisoners of war would continue languishing under brutal domination. One way or the other, the British Empire's accounts with Japan needed to be squared, and the British Pacific Fleet proved to be the weapon that did it.

FURTHER READING

Friedman, Norman, *Naval Anti-Aircraft Guns and Gunnery* (Naval Institute Press, Annapolis, MD, 2014)

Halsey, Fleet Admiral William F., *Admiral Halsey's Story* (McGraw-Hill, London, 1947)

Heckman, Neil M., 'England's Shadow Fleet: White Ensign in the Pacific' in *Sea Classics* (May 2004)

Herder, Brian Lane, *The Naval Siege of Japan: War Plan Orange Triumphant* (Osprey Publishing, Oxford, 2020)

Herder, Brian Lane, *East China Sea 1945: Climax of the Kamikaze* (Osprey Publishing, Oxford, 2022)

Hobbs, David, *Aircraft Carrier Victorious: Detailed in the Original Builders' Plans* (Naval Institute Press, Annapolis, MD, 2018)

Hobbs, David, *The British Pacific Fleet: The Royal Navy's Most Powerful Strike Force* (Seaforth Publishing, Barnsley, 2017)

Hobbs, David, *The British Pacific Fleet in 1945: A Commonwealth Effort and a Remarkable Achievement*. Available online at navy.gov.au. (Retrieved 25 June 2020)

Hobbs, David, 'The Royal Navy's Pacific Strike Force' in *Naval History Magazine* (2013) 27(1)

Konstam, Angus, *British Aircraft Carriers 1939–45* (Osprey Publishing, Oxford, 2010)

Konstam, Angus, *British Battleships 1939–45 (2): Nelson and King George V Classes* (Osprey Publishing, Oxford, 2009)

Konstam, Angus, *British Light Cruisers 1939–45* (Osprey Publishing, Oxford, 2012)

Matloff, Maurice, *Strategic Planning for Coalition Warfare 1943–1944.* (US Army, The War Department, 1960)

MacKay, Ron, *Fleet Air Arm: British Carrier Aviation 1939–1945* (Squadron-Signal Publications, Texas, 2001)

Morison, Samuel E., *Victory in the Pacific 1945* (2001)

Rawling, Bill, *A Lonely Ambassador: HMCS Uganda and the War in the Pacific*

Reynolds, Clark, *The Fast Carriers: The Forging of an Air Navy* (Naval Institute Press, Annapolis, MD, 1992)

Roskill, Stephen, *The War at Sea, Volume III, Part 2: The Offensive 1 June 1944–14 August 1945* (2009)

Sarantakes, Nicholase, 'The Short but Brilliant Life of the British Pacific Fleet' in *Joint Force Quarterly* (December 2006)

Smith, Peter C., *Task Force 57: The British Pacific Fleet, 1944–45* (Crecy Publishing Ltd, Manchester, 2001)

Vian, Sir Philip, *Action this Day: A War Memoir* (Frederick Muller Ltd, London, 1960)

Websites:

http://pwencycl.kgbudge.com/
https://www.armouredcarriers.com/
http://www.navweaps.com/
https://www.navy.gov.au/

INDEX

Note: Page locators in **bold** refer to captions, plates and pictures.